PASSENGER STEA
OF THE
RIVER FAL

Alan Kittridge

The *New Resolute* lying off the Prince of Wales Pier with M V *Miranda* of the Flushing Ferry, behind. At the pier are moored the *Roseland* and the *Victor* (behind). On the opposite side of the pier the funnels of the *Princess Victoria* and the *Queen of the Fal* can be seen. Amongst the shipping in Falmouth Harbour is the training ship *Foudroyant*, currently the subject of a restoration programme in Hartlepool. Other vessels include a trading ketch behind the *Victor*, a pilot cutter and a spritsail barge. Out in the Carrick Roads are anchored a barque and a full rigged ship. The land in the background is on the Roseland Peninsula, with St Mawes to the right. The piers and the breakwaters of Falmouth Docks can be seen on the extreme right.

Photo: E A Osborne A K collection.

Front cover: The *Victoria* of 1901 departing from Malpas.

CONTENTS

TWELVEHEADS PRESS

**Published by Twelveheads Press,
Chy Mengleth, Twelveheads,
Truro, Cornwall, TR4 8SN**

ISBN 0 906294 18 5

British Library Cataloguing - in - Publication Data available.

INTRODUCTION

The coastal cliffs of Devon and Cornwall that stand bastion against the Atlantic gales, are littered with the wreckage of ships caught in the ocean's never ending attack. Mariners in the western approaches would have faced an even more desperate beat up-Channel had nature not broken the granite fortress at intervals to offer safe anchorage. Such havens are Dartmouth, the Kingsbridge Estuary, Plymouth Sound, Fowey and in the far west, the mightiest natural harbour of all, the Carrick Roadstead. Whilst sail reigned supreme this was the haven for which ships in the Western Ocean made. On the western shore of the Carrick Roads there grew a town offering ship repairs, victualling, chandlers and towage. Profiting from its strategic maritime position as a safe anchorage for ships awaiting sailing instructions, this town became known in oceans throughout the world as Falmouth—the port for orders.

Falmouth's past importance in maritime communications might be gauged both from the number of shore based shipping agents and from the types of vessels with which the port was once associated; the famous Post Office Packets, the local watermens' quay punts and since the mid-19th century, the ubiquitous Falmouth steam tugs. In addition to local towage these tugs also served as harbour tenders, boarding craft, salvage vessels and, more importantly to the subject of this book, as passenger steamers.

A steady increase in the local population and a growth in the number of visitors, following the arrival of the railway in 1865, prompted some tug owners to introduce purpose built steamers, fully equipped for passenger comfort, retaining a towage capability as a secondary facility only. This dual role was not unique to the Fal, but nowhere else in Britain did passenger-tugs so completely dominate ferry and excursion services.

The story of the River Fal's passenger steamers does not lend itself to neat chronological summary. Neither is their history one of straightforward competition and takeover, it was more a succession of local ventures, partnerships, family alliances and amalgamations. Likewise the water they plied defies simple generalisation. Until 1939 the passenger-tug fleets continued to maintain local steamer services and excursions upon the extensive system of rivers and creeks which radiate off the Carrick Roads. It has been estimated that some sixty miles of navigable waterways lay within the ports of Falmouth and Truro. The Fal's steamers plied upon many of these reaches, some now virtually deserted. They also steamed along the entire South Cornwall coast, landing at coves and jetties that demanded an intimate knowledge of these potentially treacherous waters.

In recent years the River Tamar, on Cornwall's eastern boundary, has become the subject of much industrial, social and maritime research. Similar studies of the equally interesting Fal however remain meagre in comparison. The Fal's distinctive passenger-tugs represent only a small part of the estuary's history, a wealth of industrial and maritime research still awaits the attention of historians.

Percuil, c1900. The St Mawes ferry steamer *Roseland* lies at anchor while passengers for Gerrans are rowed ashore. The barquentiine *Bessie Dodd* has been careened on the shore for the purpose of re-caulking, repairing and cleaning. Her copper sheathing can be seen below the waterline. The *Bessie Dodd* was lost on the Newfoundland Banks in 1903. Behind the *Roseland* is Trewince Quay, which served Trewince Farm, in Porth Creek.

Royal Institution of Cornwall

CHAPTER ONE
THE WATERWAYS
AND
EARLY STEAMBOATS
OF THE
RIVER FAL

It is expedient to adopt the casual but widely recognised application of the title—River Fal, encompassing as it does much of the tidal water between St Anthony Head and the heads of navigation of the various creeks and rivers in the Falmouth and Truro districts. The advantage of employing this generalisation becomes apparent upon studying maps of the many individual tidal waterways in the area. Each river, creek, inlet and reach bears its own title, some of which have alternative spellings, or, in some instances, boast a number of completely different names. Even the Fal itself acquires an additional title once it touches the tide at Ruan Lanihorne. To help clarify both nomenclature and geography, the course of the River Fal will be traced throughout this chapter and the navigable rivers and creeks that either join it *en route* or converge with it upon the Carrick Roadstead, will each be identified.

THE PORT OF TRURO

THE RIVER FAL AND THE RUAN RIVER

Rising on Goss Moor near Roche, the water of the Fal embarks upon its twenty mile journey to the sea in Falmouth Bay. Salt water once greeted the freshwater Fal as far upstream as Tregony, or even a quarter of mile higher at a place once called Holbert or Halbot, near the present day Golden Mill. Tregony once served as a medieval inland port until the sea began retreating. By 1600 the tide flowed only to the woods above Ruan Lanihorne, about a mile below Tregony. During the late 17th century, Charles Trevanion sought to make the Fal navigable as far as Trenowth, about one mile above Grampound. By means of locks and sluices that he constructed, some boats did succeed in navigating the river a mile higher than formerly. But the scheme, which was beset with legal problems, failed when floods washed away the sluices. Until the sett bridge was built at Ruan in 1740, barges could still reach a small quay half a mile upstream which served nearby Penvose Farm. Just below Ruan Bridge the narrow Fal flows into a wide and beautiful estuary known as the Ruan River, a name bestowed upon this stretch by mariners, as Ruan Lanihorne lies near the head of navigation.

The village itself is situated along a further short, now silted, creek, but a small stone quay which served the local community still stands at its mouth, adjacent to the Tresillian Road. From this quay during the early 1900s, W.S. Blamey ran his passenger steam launch, the *Amy*, to Truro on Wednesdays and Saturdays—Truro's market days. Thus the residents of this remote district were saved the long walk to Truro, via the Malpas Ferry. In the years immediately after the First World War, Charles Henderson, in his book *Old Cornish Bridges*, noted that the estuary was becoming rapidly choked above Ardevora Veor (or Vear)—a peninsula formed by a meander of the river—rendering the remaining stretch of the navigable river accessible only to small boats which could thread their way through to the grass grown quay at Ruan. Just such a small motor boat did indeed thread its way through, and continued to do so for a number of years between the wars, providing a limited passenger service to Truro upon this idyllic stretch of water. The lonely quay in its beautiful setting remains navigable at high tide but only to the smallest of boats.

At Tregothnan, three miles below Ruan, the quiet Fal converges with the comparatively bustling Truro River and today remains virtually unnoticed by summer visitors aboard the various pleasure craft *en route* between Falmouth, Malpas and Truro.

TRURO

Visitors approaching Truro by water during the 19th century viewed a very different scene from that which presents itself today. The water frontage along the final reach of the Truro River, including the two short, navigable stretches of the Rivers Kenwyn and Allen, was tightly packed with rows of warehouses, timber yards and quayside buildings. Schooners, trading ketches and river barges worked the very limit of salt water, resting at mud berths to unload their cargoes onto Garras Wharf and Lemon and Town Quays along the Kenwyn, or directly into the warehouses of Trafalgar (now Phoenix) Wharf on the River Allen. Schooners at Trafalgar Wharf virtually wedged themselves into the narrow inlet adjacent to the passenger steamer landing place at Worth's Quay. The tide once met the Kenwyn as it emerged beneath Lemon Street Bridge, but sadly, since 1923, this part of the river has remained covered over to provide car parking space. Thus reduced to an underground stream, the Kenwyn emerges from its subterranean course beneath Truro only briefly before it slips silently into the Truro River.

The first, Truro-owned, passenger steamer to operate on the waters of the Fal appears to have been the 66·5ft* long, wooden paddle steamer *Dart*. Built at North Shields by Andrew Bell in 1836, she was fitted with three lugger rigged masts and a bowsprit. As befits her name, she was originally operated upon the River Dart in South Devon. On 13th December 1841, she was purchased by William Mansell Tweedy, Humphrey Williams and Edward Turner, all bankers and also Trustees of the Truro and Falmouth Steam Packet Company. It seems likely that this venture was promoted by William Tweedy to link Truro with the Falmouth & Southampton Steam Packet Company's coastal paddle steamer, the *Lord Beresford*, in which he was also a shareholder. Neither service seems to have met with success. Within months the Truro company was wound up, although the *Dart* appears to have continued the river link until the Falmouth & Southampton Steam Packet Company also withdrew their service in the spring of 1843. During the same year, W.M. Tweedy and others promoted the Cornwall Railway which eventually linked the West Cornwall Railway from Penzance to the South Devon at Plymouth.

Over thirty years were to elapse before another passenger steamer was entered onto the Port of Truro Shipping Register*. In 1877, during the same year that Truro was designated a City, Richard Benney, the Truro River pilot, took delivery of a new wooden, screw, steam tug named the *Resolute*. She measured 63·6 x 14·25 x 6·31ft (length x breadth x depth) and was carvel built by William Scoble and John Davies at their shipyard, downriver at Malpas. Her original engine was built by Nicholas Sara's foundry at Penryn, but in 1886 was replaced by a new unit supplied by Cox & Co. of Falmouth. Richard Benney owned half of her sixty four shares• and was designated as Managing Owner. His brother, James Cornelius Benney of Falmouth, a master mariner, took eight shares and was appointed as Master. Messrs Scoble and Davies also accepted eight shares each as part payment for her construction. Charles Ralph Gatley, a gentleman of Truro, provided the only outside capital by taking up the remaining eight shares.

---

* An Act of Parliament in 1786 called for the registration of all ships 'having a deck, or being of 15 tons or upwards'.

• The system of dividing the ownership in every British merchant ship into sixty-four shares was adopted by Act of Parliament in 1824.

---

*' An Act of Parliament in 1836 introduced feet and decimal measurements, replacing feet and inches.

To augment the revenue gained from towing ships on the Truro River, Richard Benney obtained a certificate to carry 70 passengers within the confines of the Ports of Truro and Falmouth. The distinctive tricolour funnel adopted for Benney and Co's steamer—red and white with a black top—was to remain a feature of the Fal for over sixty years, as Benney & Co. built up a small fleet of similar passenger-tugs which were later owned and operated by the River Fal Steamship Co.Ltd.

THE TRURO AND TRESILLIAN RIVERS

The tortuous channel of the Truro River's shallow upper limits meanders from bank to bank almost all the way to Malpas. The waterside houses of Trennick Row are passed on the eastern shore, so too is Sunny Corner, where Charles Dyer once built schooners and barges on the beach beside the Malpas Road. The shallow Calenick Creek on the opposite shore was navigated by barges serving the smelting works, rope walk and corn mill at its head, in the village of Calenick. There was also a small boatyard near Calenick Quay.

Schooners and ketches once left the slipway at Scoble and Davies' shipyard, which clung to the river bank below Malpas. In addition to building Benney & Co's steamer, the *Resolute*, Messrs Scoble and Davies also launched her fleet sister, the passenger-tug *New Resolute* in 1882, once again taking up eight shares each. William Scoble was occasionally employed as engineer aboard the *New Resolute* during the decade after her launch.

At the village of Malpas, the ferryman could be called upon to fulfil his obligation of ferrying passengers across the mouth of the Tresillian River to Malpas Passage, in the parish of St Michael Penkevil, or over to Kea on the western bank of the Truro River. A horse and wagon boat was also available until the late 1920s. During 1858, Malpas was served by the coastal steamer *Albatross*, which called twice weekly to land her Truro-bound passengers. She was owned by William West, the iron founder of St Blazey, and chartered during 1858 and part of 1859 by the Par Steamship Company. For the Par company the *Albatross* maintained a coastal packet service between Plymouth, Fowey, Par and Malpas—for

Truro. The Par Steamship Company had, since 1854, successfully operated their wooden paddler, the *Forager*, on weekly passages between Plymouth and Fowey. Her shareholders numbered up to twenty three and included Lieut. William Foulkes Essel, R.N. and Rev. Edward John Treffry of Fowey. The *Albatross* was withdrawn and the Par Steamship Company dissolved when, in May 1859, Brunel's Royal Albert Bridge, which spans the River Tamar, was opened and the Cornwall Railway from Truro was finally linked to the Plymouth-Paddington mainlines.

The village of Malpas and the cottages at Malpas Passage face each other across the mouth of the broad, but shallow, Tresillian River, which continues along its tree lined course for a further three miles to the head of navigation at the village of Tresillian, the highest tidal limit on the Fal estuary. Tresillian Quay today serves as a Cornwall County Council highway maintenance depot. Road stone was once collected by river barges from quarries at Porthoustock, on the Lizard Peninsula. The barges unloaded the stone beside the Truro Road, at Tresillian Quay, to be collected by lorries. The last barge to engage in this trade was the Plymouth built *Shamrock*, which was plying to Tresillian as late as the 1960s. The *Shamrock* is now preserved by the National Trust and the National Maritime Museum and moored at Cotehele Quay on the River Tamar. Passenger steamers occasionally plied the Tresillian River. Such excursions were made near high tide and either turned two miles upstream from Malpas, at Pencalenick, without landing, or made their way right up to Tresillian to land their passengers at Gatley's Quay.

Continuing down the Truro River from Malpas, the channel increases considerably, both in width and depth. Timber ships too large to ply into Truro itself, anchored along this stretch off Woodbury (or Woodberry) and Maggoty Bank, while lightermen from Coombe, Malpas and Truro loaded their river lighters or built huge rafts of timber which were towed and poled upstream to Harvey's timber yard at Truro.

One and a half miles below Malpas at Tregothnan, seat of Lord Falmouth, the River Fal is joined.

THE RIVER FAL AND THE COOMBE, RESTRONGUET & MYLOR CREEKS

The ancient ferry at Tolverne once provided the most convenient passenger link between Tolverne Passage on the Truro side and Tolverne Cottage on the opposite Roseland Peninsula shore. Peter Newman's 37ft motor launch, the *Heather*, currently lands passengers from Falmouth at Tolverne Cottage, for morning coffee, lunch or cream teas. Peter Newman's father, Rodney, took over the ferry cottage in the 1930s and maintained the ferry to Tolverne Passage until the Second World War. During the 1940s and 50s, Rodney Newman and his son George established a fleet of passenger launches on the Fal. Each bore the name *Skylark*. The flagship of this little fleet was the 63·9ft *Skylark of Tolverne*, the last passenger boat to be entered onto the Truro Register.

On the west bank of the Fal, opposite Tolverne, are the creeks of Coombe (or Cowlands) and Leemouth (or Lamouth). Upon the point of land where the creeks divide stands Roundwood Quay, once owned by R.A. Daniell, a wealthy Truro merchant with considerable local mining interests. During the first half of the 19th century the mineral trade from this quay declined, against the corresponding growth of the Devoran Quays in Restronguet Creek. The shipbuilder, Henry Stephens Trethowan, of Little Falmouth, utilised the quay as a secondary shipyard in the 1880s. The steamers of Benney & Co. called at Roundwood, alias the 'Plum Gardens', at the turn of the century and passengers disembarked to enjoy the local Kea plums.

The fifty foot depth of water that is available at low tide in the Tolverne and King Harry Reaches of the Fal, has rendered these beautiful stretches of river an ideal lay up berth for redundant ocean going shipping. The striking scene created by the presence of rows of immense ships lying silently at moorings laid out along the sylvan scenery of King Harry Reach, has surprised unsuspecting visitors for many years. Notable amongst these mothballed vessels have been the White Star liner, the *Laurentic* and the cruisers, HMS *Leander* and HMS *Ajax*. Shaw Savil's liner, the *Southern Cross*, and the two Cunarders,

the *Franconia* and the *Carmania*, created an unforgettable sight in 1971-2 when they were all laid up at the same time, downstream of the King Harry Ferry. The most recent 'celebrity' was the British India liner and Falklands Task Force hospital ship, the SS *Uganda*.

The King Harry Ferry which crosses the Fal between the Feock and Philleigh districts, was, until September 1889, maintained by a horse boat, similar to that employed at Malpas. In 1888, the King Harry Steam Ferry Co. Ltd was incorporated to introduce a steam chain bridge. Their first bridge, or chain ferry, was built of steel in 1889 by Messrs Sara & Burgess of Penryn.

At Turnaware Point, nearly fifteen miles from its source and five miles downstream from Truro, the River Fal flows into the massive natural haven of the Carrick Roads. Three creeks line the immediate western shore: Channals Creek, below Trelissick; Pill Creek at Feock, and Restronguet Creek. Restronguet was alternatively known as Devoran Creek, while the wharves of the Redruth & Chasewater Railway flourished at Devoran. To mariners navigating the creek to Perran Wharf, some three miles inland at Perranarworthal on the River Kennall, the waterway was referred to as the Perran River. During the 19th century this creek was subjected to a considerable burst of industrial activity. Use was made of its sheltered tidal waters to support, amongst other ventures, a foundry, mineral wharves and a shipyard, each of which played a small part in the story of the Fal's passenger steamers.

Great quantities of Welsh coal and Scandinavian timber were landed at Perran Wharf in the 18th century, much of it destined for the mining districts of the Carnon Valley. The Fox family of Falmouth, merchants with major interests in the Gwennap mines, established an iron foundry at Perran Wharf in 1791. The twelve partners in their Perran Foundry Company were nearly all Quakers and either members of the Fox family or linked through family alliances. The group was headed by George Croker Fox, a Falmouth shipping agent, who in the previous year had purchased the house near the Customs House Quay in Falmouth that remains today as the offices of G.C. Fox & Co., Shipping Agents.

In 1841, Charles Fox of the Perran Works, together with Alfred Fox of Falmouth, William Tweedy of Truro and others, purchased the wooden, coastal paddle steamer *Lord Beresford*. She was built in Bristol in 1824 by William Scott & Co. and for seventeen years maintained a service between Portsmouth and the Channel Islands. Her new Cornish owners styled themselves, the Falmouth & Southampton Steam Packet Company, and inaugurated a service between those ports calling at Mevagissey, Plymouth and Torquay. The cost of a passage for the entire trip was: 'Chief Cabin' £1.10s.; 'Fore Cabin' £1; or you could take your chance on deck for the whole trip at 12s.6d. After just two years the service was withdrawn and in May 1843 the *Lord Beresford* was sold to Joseph Price of Neath Abbey, for future use on the Bristol Channel.

Amongst the web of business connections which permeate many 18th and 19th century Cornish business ventures, the name of Price links a number of enterprises. The Price family of South Wales were Quakers and in addition to sharing their religious beliefs with the Foxes, the two families also enjoyed mutually beneficial business relationships. It was in conjunction with the Price family that the Perran Foundry was established, Peter Price being one of the partners. The Prices owned the Neath Abbey Iron Works, the lease of which was acquired by the Fox family in 1792. During 1828 Joseph Price chartered his steam packet, the *Bristol*, to the Plymouth & Portsmouth Steam Packet Company. For this company she maintained a packet service between Falmouth, Mevagissey, Charlestown, Fowey and Plymouth. At Plymouth she linked with the packet company's paddle steamers, the *Sir Francis Drake* and the *Brunswick*, which were maintaining Portsmouth and Channel Island runs. In 1866 Henry Habberley Price of Neath Abbey Iron Works built the iron, screw, passenger-tug *Wotton* for Howard and Robert Fox of Falmouth. Details of this steamer and of her career at Falmouth appear in Chapter Two.

The Perran Foundry passed to the control of the Williams family of Scorrier by the mid 19th century. At this time the foundry was active in producing steam machinery for the mining and agricultural industries, but they also built some marine steam engines.* In 1869 the foundry supplied a single cylinder engine for the Truro tug *North Star*. Two years later a similar unit was ordered by Joseph Osborne of Newquay, who was building a wooden, screw, passenger steamer, the *Jane*, which was later owned by the St Mawes Steam Tug & Passenger Co.Ltd. In 1876, 1877 and 1878 three successive two cylinder units were built by the foundry for the Falmouth tug owner, Philip Thomas. Each engine was fitted to successive tugs named *Albert*; all three vessels were built speculatively, profits from each sale financing the next construction. Speculative building ventures and the subsequent renaming of each successive vessel with the same name became endemic to the history of Falmouth's towage and passenger steamer trades, adding much to the confusion of future historians! The first two *Albert* tugs were iron hulled and were built by Cox, Farley & Co. of Falmouth. The third was built of wood in 1879 by John Stephens of Devoran at Yard Point, Feock, just inside the mouth of Restronguet Creek.

The Stephens shipyard flourished between 1859 and 1879, building schooners and ketches to the design of William Ferris. In addition to the *Albert*, the yard also built the Truro tug *North Star*, noted above. William Ferris' brother, Peter, left Yard Point in 1870 to become the head man at the newly-acquired yard of John Stephens of Charlestown, who was apparently unrelated to the Devoran Stephens'. In 1872, from the little yard at the back of Charlestown Dock, Peter Ferris launched the 67ft wooden, passenger-tug *Rapid*, for Philip Thomas of Falmouth.

Near the wooded shoreline below Carclew, Restronguet Creek divides. The River Kennall, or the Perran River, channel follows a westerly course to Perranarworthal, whilst a second channel continues on a north-westerly course up to the main Truro-Falmouth road (A39). This second channel is scoured

---

* The Perran Foundry buildings were converted to a mill in 1897. At the time of writing there are proposals for the restoration of the buildings with multiple use, including an industrial museum element and a Perran Foundry Trust is being established.

out of the muddy creek bed by the Carnon River, which rises near Scorrier and flows through the mining districts of St Day, Twelveheads and Bissoe. The channel proved of little use to the Redruth & Chasewater Railway Company, which in 1824 was developing quays near Devoran and Point to serve as a terminus for their 4ft gauge mineral railway and provide moorings for the anticipated shipping. Whilst a narrow channel did exist alongside the tin and copper smelting works at Point, in Penpol Creek, the more suitable waterside site at Devoran was served only by a drying tidal berth, located some yards north of the main Carnon channel. A proposed floating harbour failed to materialise, instead the railway company built new wharves below Narabo Farm, immediately downstream of Devoran itself. To maintain sufficient depth of water for vessels of 200 tons the existing tidal channel to Devoran and that alongside the wharves, was regularly scoured by releasing water from a reservoir sluice, which the Company built upstream from Devoran. However, the channel still required extensive dredging throughout the Company's history. Ironically, most of the silt originated from the very same mines that the railway was built to serve.

In 1847 the Redruth & Chasewater Railway Company acquired a paddle tug, the *Sydney*, to improve the efficiency of their harbour by towing vessels in and out of the creek, vessels which otherwise might have remained wind or tidebound. The *Sydney* was registered in Falmouth on 25th October 1848. She measured 80t.g. (tons gross)*, 80·7 x 15·5 x 9ft and had been built in Middlesborough in 1841. She was registered in the ownership of Richard Taylor of Falmouth, who held all 64 of her shares. Richard was the son of John Taylor, an enormously successful mining adventurer with interests in Tamar Valley mines and the mighty Consolidated Mines in the Gwennap District. John Taylor was also the promoter, a director, and had originally been the Manager of, the Redruth & Chasewater Railway. After 1850 Richard Taylor took charge of the Railway and

the Cornish mining interests of John Taylor & Sons. During her first year of operation, under the command of Capt.John Tregaskis, the Sydney earned a small profit. But for the following three successive years she required a series of extensive repairs. Decking renewals, hull doubling and new boilers were all included in the list of work undertaken during 1849—1851. In an attempt to generate extra revenue from the paddle tug, the railway company offered a shilling in the pound bonus to her Captain and Engineer, of any profit the tug could make during the course of a year. It is possibly at this time, during the mid 1850s, that her master applied for a Class 3 passenger certificate*. This certificate is noted by the late Graham Farr in his book, *Westcountry Passenger Steamers*, but other reference to the *Sydney*'s passenger trade has yet to come to light. It is recorded, however, that she underwent extensive alterations in Liverpool in 1857, during which time passenger facilities might have been added or improved.

D.B. Barton in his history of the railway, records the purchase of a second paddle tug, the *Pendennis*, in 1858. She was fitted with 'Stewart's patent mud rakes' to assist in the ever present problem of dredging the Devoran channel. The *Pendennis* was not registered in Falmouth or Truro and further details of the tug are difficult to trace. D.B. Barton's account infers that this vessel and the *Pendennis* that survived on the Fal until 1876 are one and the same. However, a second *Pendennis* was launched from Charles Lungley's yard at Deptford, on the

---

* The Steamboat Act of 1819 established registration and inspection of all passenger carrying steam vessels by officers of the Board of Trade. Following the Steamboat Act of 1851 all steamboats had to be surveyed twice a year and the number of passengers carried was controlled by a certificate. The main certification classes relevant to the history of the River Fal's passenger steamers are: Class 2 Home Trade—crossings to Continental ports within the Elbe-Brest limits.

Class 3 Sea going witin specified limits.

Class 4 River services within a strictly defined semi- smooth water area.

Class 5 Harbour, estuary and river services on smooth water.

---

* The calculated tonnage of machinery spaces when added to the ship's net or registered tonnage gives the gross tonnage (t.g.).

Thames, on 27th June 1863. She was a 73·32t.g.*, iron framed paddle tug, measuring 79·4 x 16·9 x 8·9ft and was powered by two side lever engines built by John Stewart of Blackwall (perhaps the same Stewart who's patent mud rakes were fitted to the first *Pendennis*). Her owner was Richard Taylor, who once again held all of her shares. Following the arrival of the *Pendennis* in 1863, Taylor formed the Port of Falmouth Steam Tug Co.Ltd. to manage both the *Sydney* and the new vessel. The *Sydney* was transferred to the ownership of the new Company and in 1870 was sold to foreign owners. On July 2nd of the same year, the *Falmouth Packet* newspaper carried the following advertisement:

> 'Port of Falmouth Steam Tug Co.Ltd ..... owners of the *Pendennis* steam boat having complied with all provisions of law for safety of passengers as certified by the Marine Department of the Board of Trade are ready to undertake excursions for pleasure parties to LIZARD, KYNANCE COVE, FOWEY, PLYMOUTH or other places within these limits ... apply to Nathaniel Hayes, 15 Wellington Terrace, Falmouth.'

The Port of Falmouth Steam Tug Co.Ltd in fact acted only as agents or managers for the *Pendennis*, as her registered ownership remained in the name of her sole shareholder, Richard Taylor, until 15th December 1876, when she was sold to Philip Thomas of Falmouth. Her sale ended the Redruth & Chasewater Railway Company's links with the local towage and excursion trades, albeit a tenuous one at this date. Philip Thomas resold the *Pendennis* within six months to Henry H. Englis, of Peterborough.

Due south from Restronguet Point lies the final tidal inlet in the Port of Truro, the shallow, short, Mylor Creek, along which the tide reaches Mylor Bridge at its head. Mylor Creek is notable for the small Admiralty Dockyard which occupied a site in Mylor Pool, at the mouth of the creek. Associated with this dockyard between 1865 and 1899 was the 'wooden wall' naval training ship, HMS *Ganges*, which was moored

---

* In 1855 an Act of Parliament adopted a decimal system for tonnage measurement replacing fractions of ¹/₃₅₀₀ths of a ton. Official numbers were also introduced.

in St Just Pool on the opposite shore of the Carrick Roads. It was the departure of HMS *Ganges* which signalled the dockyard's demise as a naval base. The substantial stone jetties survive today as part of Mylor Yacht Harbour. The steamers of both Benney & Co. and the St Mawes Steam Tug & Passenger Co.Ltd visited the creek, usually turning off Trelew without landing. However, special calls were made to visit the annual Mylor Regatta. In 1906 Mr P. Bell's motor launch, the *Ibis*—probably the first internal combustion engined passenger boat on the Fal—offered morning and afternoon cruises to Mylor. The afternoon call landed at the old dockyard jetties for Mrs Copp's Mylor Refreshment Rooms, near Mylor Church, where Cornish clotted cream teas were served.

THE PORT OF FALMOUTH

THE CARRICK ROADS & THE PENRYN RIVER

At Penarrow Point, on the shore of the Carrick Roads, immediately south of Mylor Pool, stands an obelisk. A similar monolith, sited on the opposite shore of the Roadstead at Messack Point in St Just Pool, lines up to mark the seaward limit of the Port of Truro. Truro once held jurisdiction over virtually the entire Fal estuary, excepting only the Port of Penryn. In 1652, Penryn's Customs House was moved to the growing town of Smithwick and in 1660, Charles II declared that henceforth this town should be known as Falmouth. Since 1661, Falmouth has exercised port rights on the Fal estuary, granted by Charles II and the two obelisks on the Carrick Roads remain to mark the division between the port authorities. The positions of these obelisks were suitably chosen, marking as they do the confluence of the River Fal's channel into the deep water sound of the Carrick Roads at St Just Pool. Upstream from the boundary stones the unbroken expanse of surface water covers the ria, or drowned river valley of the Fal. Whilst the main channel to Turnaware remains deep at all states of the tide, the massive mud banks flanking it on either side can lie a mere 2ft beneath the surface of the water at low tide. John Leland, writing in the 1530s, described the

Carrick Roads as, 'a haven very notable and famous and in a manner the most principal of all Britayne'. Richard Carew in 1602 noted 'a hundred sail of vessels may anchor in it and not one see the mast of another'. The sheltered deep water anchorage was a haven for sailing ships in the Western Approaches and for coastal vessels navigating the English Channel. Through shipping agents like G.C. Fox in Falmouth, ships could fix a cargo in another port, or receive their next sailing orders. In 1688 the port was designated as a Post Office Packet Station for the Spanish Mails and for over two centuries prospered from its strategic maritime position.

At the tidal head of the Penryn River stands the old market town and ancient Port of Penryn. Although its maritime importance was largely eclipsed by the growth of the adjacent Port of Falmouth, evidence of Penryn's continued waterborne trade, well into the 20th century, still survives in the shape of now-redundant warehouses and silent quays. During the 19th century and early 20th centuries the port relied greatly upon both the export of Penryn granite, from the nearby quarries of Freeman, Sons & Co Ltd., and a trade in shipping live cattle from Corunna. At the very head of navigation in Penryn, on the site currently occupied by Kessel's Garage, Nicholas Sara, an ex-foreman at the Perran Foundry, established his own foundry. He built the engine for Benney's *Resolute* in 1877. In 1887 his son, Evan Burnett Sara, and John Burgess, also from the Perran Foundry, took over the company and built the first King Harry chain ferry in 1889.

On the northern shore of the Penryn River, opposite Falmouth, lies the village of Flushing. Once known as Nankersey, tradition suggests that the village gained its present title from Dutch engineers employed by the Trefusis family to build the sea wall and quays that survive today. It is with the history of the Post Office packets that this waterside community is most closely associated.

The Port of Falmouth was appointed as a station for the Corunna and Lisbon Post Office packets in 1688. The West Indies and New York packet contracts were awarded in 1702 and 1755 respectively. Between 1705 and the 1720s, Samuel Trefusis gained

the packet agency and transferred some of the trade to his quays at Flushing. In 1709 he built a warehouse for the packet service near the present day Flushing Old Quay. Many houses in the village owe their existence to the packet trade, being either owned or occupied by masters and men of the Falmouth Packets. A plaque mounted upon the sole remaining wall of Samuel Trefusis' warehouse, known as the Great Cellars, commemorates Flushing's connections with the Packet Service. In 1823, responsibility for the packet contracts was transferred from the Post Office to the Admiralty and within a decade they were using their own Naval steamers on the Lisbon service. The remaining Falmouth contracts were soon won by the new transatlantic steamship companies working out of Southampton.

Some of the Falmouth packets were built on the slipway of the Shipwrights Yard, at Little Falmouth, just along the shore from Flushing. It was perhaps from the yard that the River Fal's first locally-built steamer was launched in 1831. Registered as Flushing built, this 24t.g. wooden paddle steamer, the *Alert*, measured 46·3 x 10·1 x 6·5ft. She was decorated with a 'woman bust' figurehead and owned by Captain John Brewer, a mariner of Flushing. These few details, taken from her entry in Falmouth Customs House Shipping Register, remain as the sole evidence I have seen concerning the history of this steamer at Falmouth. In his book, *Westcountry Passenger Steamers*, Graham Farr suggests her use as a market boat or river packet on the Fal estuary. She was sold in 1836 to Captain John Rickard of Calstock. Throughout her subsequent career on the River Tamar, she was indeed used as a river packet. Until she was broken up in 1856, the *Alert* provided a service linking both Admiral's Hard, in Stonehouse and Devonport's Mutton Cove, to Calstock and other landings along the navigable upper.stretches of the River Tamar.

FALMOUTH – COASTAL PACKETS

The earliest steamships to visit Falmouth were local coastal and Irish steam packets. Since 1826 the PS *Erin* and the PS *Shannon* plied between Belfast and London, calling at Falmouth, Plymouth and other south coast ports. The PS *Shannon* belonged to the

British & Irish Steam Packet Company and enjoyed a long association with Falmouth, calling until 1846. Other Irish packets maintaining this passenger service included the paddle steamers *William Fawcett*, *Thames* and *City of Londonderry*. The Irish packets undoubtedly improved South Cornwall's communications and transport links with Plymouth, Portsmouth, Southampton and London, but they were not alone in providing such services. From Hill's Shipyard at Cattedown, Plymouth in 1823, the 113t.n. wooden paddler *Sir Francis Drake* was launched. She measured 103ft 8ins x 18ft 8ins x 11ft 0ins and was amongst the first steamers to be built on the South Devon and South Cornwall coast. It was along this coast that she was to ply for thirty five years, during which time she became a familiar sight and a regular visitor to Falmouth.

The *Sir Francis Drake* was built to the order of a group of Plymouth shareholders, who styled themselves the Plymouth & Portsmouth Steam Packet Company. Initially it was between these two ports that the steamer plied. During 1824, however, the opportunity was taken by Bristol Channel packet operators, John and William Jones, to introduce a steamer running between Falmouth, Fowey and Plymouth, to link with the *Sir Francis Drake*'s Portsmouth run. In the spring of 1824 the Jones' sent their 48t.n., 71ft wooden paddler, the *Royal Cambria*, around to Falmouth, probably the first steamer to visit the port. The *Royal Cambria* maintained the service throughout the year and was substituted in 1825 by a slightly longer paddle steamer, the 79ft *St David*. This second steamer landed her passengers at the newly constructed Admiral's Hard, in Stonehouse Pool. An additional call was made off Mevagissey, with local boatmen ferrying passengers between ship and shore. The *St David* performed three round trips per week, but within the year the service was discontinued and the steamer returned to her original Newport-Bristol route. Her early departure was signalled by the Plymouth & Portsmouth Steam Packet Company's decision to correct their oversight in omitting Falmouth from their original schedule. Their new service inaugurated towards the end of 1825, was achieved by extending the *Sir Francis Drake*'s winter season runs to include calls at Fowey, Charlestown, Mevagissey and Falmouth. Her ports of call east of Plymouth included Dartmouth, Brixham, Torquay and Teignmouth. In July 1826, the Plymouth & Portsmouth Steam Packet Company introduced a second steamer to the route. The new vessel was a wooden paddle steamer measuring 218t.n. and 128ft 6ins long. She was built at Rotherhithe and named the *Brunswick*.

During 1829 the Plymouth & Portsmouth Steam Packet Company attempted to improve their Channel Islands packet services from Plymouth and Portsmouth by using both of their steamers on the Islands routes. To maintain the Falmouth-Plymouth link they chartered Joseph Price's Bristol Channel steam packet, the *Bristol*. The *Sir Francis Drake* was sold in 1829 to Captain Thomas Ward of Falmouth, who later sold 32 shares to Captain James Mill of the *Brunswick*. Both steamers however remained under the Plymouth & Portsmouth Steam Packet Company banner. It was the *Sir Francis Drake* that in 1832 brought Falmouth news of the passing of the Reform Bill. The overland mail took a further 24 hours to provide Truro with the details. Captain Thomas Ward took command of a new packet, the 94t.n. *Cornubia*, in 1832. She was owned by the Plymouth, Falmouth & Penzance Steam Packet Company to maintain services between those ports and the Channel Islands.

In 1841, the Falmouth & Southampton Steam Packet Company, namely Charles Fox of Perran Foundry, William Tweedy of Truro and Alfred Fox, Joseph Winn and William Reynolds, each of Falmouth, purchased the ex-Portsmouth-Channel Islands steam packet, the *Lord Beresford*. She was a wooden paddler measuring 117t.n., 117ft 11ins x 18ft 2ins x 11ft 9ins. Built in 1824, she was named after the Governor of Jersey. As noted earlier in this chapter, the Falmouth & Southampton Steam Packet Company's service, which called at Mevagissey, Plymouth, Torquay and Southampton, was withdrawn after two years. The company might have been prompted into their venture following the tragic loss of the Irish packet *Thames* during January 1841, when she foundered and broke up on the Western Rocks of the Isles of Scilly, with the loss of 60 lives. However, competition was still forthcoming from either the *Sir Francis Drake* or the *Brunswick* and the Irish packet, the *Shannon*. The *Lord Beresford* was sold to Joseph Price of the Neath Abbey Iron Works. The long-serving *Shannon* suffered a serious fire at Plymouth in 1846. Although there was no loss of life, the fire effectively ended the paddler's career in English waters.

For a further fifteen years, the *Brunswick*, until 1855, and then the *Sir Francis Drake*, alone continued the coastal steam packet link, until on 4th May 1859 the first railway train crossed Brunel's Royal Albert Bridge at Saltash. Thus the West Cornwall railway lines were linked to those of the South Devon, Bristol & Exeter and the Great Western, providing a direct link between Penzance and Paddington, albeit with a break of gauge at Truro. The coastal steam packet service had been withdrawn at the end of the previous year and the *Sir Francis Drake* sold to a Sidmouth owner. Steamers of the British & Irish Steam Packet Co.Ltd continued to call at Falmouth *en route* between Ireland and London. In 1938 the Company merged with Coast Lines Ltd. The origins of Coast Lines Ltd is found in the Liverpool-Bristol-Falmouth-Plymouth-Southampton-London services maintained by the steamers of the Powell, Bacon and Hough Lines, themselves once regular callers to Falmouth.

The long awaited railway line which connected Falmouth to the mainline at Truro opened in August 1863. Stations were provided at Perran (renamed Perranwell in 1864), Penryn and Falmouth. Under the original Act of 1846 the line was to terminate at Greenbank, near Falmouth's town centre. But a subsequent alteration to this Act in 1861 allowed a deviation along higher ground to terminate the line near the new Falmouth Docks.

The railway's arrival sparked a number of schemes to cater for visitors. The waterfront facing Falmouth Bay soon acquired some of the trappings to be found in fashionable seaside resorts. The Falmouth Hotel was completed in 1865, followed by a succession of villas and hotels built along the immediate Falmouth Bay foreshore. The scenic Castle Drive was also opened

in 1865, providing sweeping views of Falmouth, St-Mawes, the Carrick Roads and Falmouth Bay. During the 1870s, Gyllyngvase Beach was developed by the Corporation, resulting in the foreshore and pleasure gardens that survive today. The warm climate enjoyed in Falmouth Bay was promoted in publicity material. Favourable statistics were produced, highlighting the year round mild temperatures. Palm trees were planted to enhance a 'Riviera' image which was later promoted to great effect by the G.W.R. To cater for increasing numbers of middle class visitors, wealthy new residents in St Mawes and Flushing and the growing local population, fleets of passenger steamers were established, both to provide local services and to offer 'healthful' river and coastal excursions.

In tandem with the growth of Falmouth's resort, overlooking Falmouth Bay, the arrival of the railway further encouraged the development of the town's

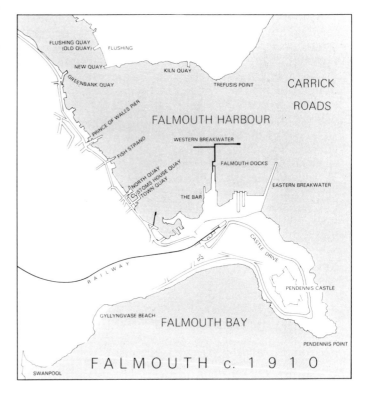

FALMOUTH c. 1910

port facilities in Falmouth Harbour. In 1864 a junction was made to connect the line with the Falmouth Dock Company's own railway system. The foundation stone of Falmouth Docks was laid in 1860 and the Prince of Wales Breakwater (now Eastern Breakwater), Western Wharf and No.1 Dry Dock were completed and opened by the Falmouth Docks Company in July 1861. Foremost amongst the Dock's promoters was Alfred Fox, the first Chairman of the Dock Company.

This dual dock and resort development was a contributory factor in the evolution of Falmouth's distinctive passenger-tug fleets.

FALMOUTH PASSENGER TUGS

Whilst the establishment of through rail traffic from London to Truro had resulted in the withdrawal of the local, coastal packet services, so the construction of the railway branch line to Falmouth and the development of Falmouth as a dock and a resort, in turn heralded a new era in the local towage and passenger steamer trades.

The *Sir Francis Drake*, in common with many other passenger steamers of this period, exercised a liberty to tow whilst on passenger service. Her imminent withdrawal towards the end of 1858, signalled the loss of this useful secondary facility. Edmund Handcock, a Falmouth shipowner, decided to provide a tug of his own. In April 1858 he purchased an 84t.g. wooden, paddle tug, the *Dandy*. She measured 90·8 x 17·6 x 9·25ft and had been built in South Shields during the previous year. Initially owning the paddler outright, Handcock soon sold 52 shares to twenty three other local people, included amongst which was Howard Fox of Falmouth. Five years later the *Dandy* was replaced by a larger paddle tug, also named the *Dandy*. This second steamer was built for Handcock by Marshal Bros of South Shields and measured 125·89t.g. and 105·9 x 19·1 x 9·95ft. Handcock held all 64 of her shares. Two years later, Howard Fox, in partnership with his brother Robert, placed an order with his family's Welsh business associates, the Prices of Neath Abbey, for an iron, screw tug of their own. Registered at Falmouth early in 1867, this little 28·46t.g. steamer, the *Wot-*

ton, acted as a tender and performed towage work in Falmouth Harbour. She was sold within two years to a group of St Mawes owners and once converted for full time passenger work, became the first regular passenger steamer to ply between St Mawes and Falmouth. Various members of the Fox family continued to maintain an interest in tug ownership over the years. The steam tugs *St Keverne*, *Pendragon*, *Briton* and the appropriately named *Perran*, were each owned at one time by members of the Fox family.

In 1866, a 41·58t.g., iron, screw tug, the *Dolphin*, was registered at Falmouth. She is notable in the story of the Fal's passenger steamers for her list of shareholders, rather than her purely towage operation. William Walter Sewell, an engineer, was her leading shareholder, with 32 shares. Nearly a decade later Sewell owned an iron, screw, passenger-tug named the *Victor*, built for him by Harveys of Hayle. Albert and Elizabeth Handcock later acquired 16 and 8 shares respectively in the *Victor*. This tug was a forerunner of the well known local coastal passenger steamer of the same name, which was closely associated with the River Fal Steamship Company until 1934.

London born, Philip Thomas, a master mariner of Falmouth, held 12 shares in the *Dolphin*. This appears to have been his first shareholding in a Falmouth registered steamer. In 1872 Thomas took delivery of his own 67ft long, wooden, screw passenger-tug, the *Rapid*, which was built at the John Stephens yard of Charlestown. The *Rapid* worked as a river packet between Falmouth and Truro during the summer months and sought towage work during the winter. She was sold in February 1879 to owners on the River Medway. Philip Thomas next bought and sold in quick succession a number of tugs: the wooden paddler *Lady Bute*, between 1875-1879; Richard Taylor's *Pendennis*; the three *Albert* screw tugs, noted earlier in this chapter and in 1882, an iron, screw, passenger-tug, the *Emperor*.

A third shareholder in the *Dolphin* was James Bennet who had previously brought an ex-Solent paddler, the *Duke of Buccleugh* to the district in 1859. He registered her at Penzance in 1861 and reportedly operated her at Falmouth for five years, as a tug in the winter and an excursion vessel in the summer. Bennet later owned a 38·71t.g. screw tug, the *Prairie Bird*, and seems to have restricted his subsequent steam boat interests to the towage trade only.

The fourth and final shareholder in the *Dolphin* was Elizabeth Handcock, who owned 8 shares. When the *Dolphin* was sold in 1874, Elizabeth Handcock transferred her interest to Sewell's next tug, the *Victor*.

Edmund Handcock, meanwhile, had sold his paddle tug, the *Dandy*(2), in 1871 and purchased two new steamers, a steel, screw tug, the *Laura* and a wooden, passenger, screw steamer, the *Jane*. The *Jane* was built by Joseph Osborne at his Island Cove Yard at Newquay in 1872. She was powered by an engine from the Perran Foundry and measured 16·38t.g. and 46·8 x 12·7 x 5·3ft. For four years she was operated at Newquay by Osborne. The *Jane* remained in Handcocks ownership for just two years and was sold in April 1878 to the St Mawes Steam Tug & Passenger Co.Ltd. The final involvement of the Handcock family in the River Fal's passenger steamer trade was Enos Albert Handcock's partnership with Philip Thomas in the passenger-tug *Emperor* of 1883—Thomas's second tug to bear the name. She was a 90ft iron, screw steamer built by Harvey's of Hayle. Her managing owner was Philip Thomas of Falmouth. The Master was Capt. Philip Thomas, Jnr. Between January and June the *Emperor* worked as a tug within the limits of the Port of Falmouth. During July and August she was employed mainly on coastal excursions to destinations within the limits of Penzance and Plymouth. She did venture up river sometimes and on one occasion landed a Working Men's trip at Tregothnan for the afternoon. During 1903, the Thomas family took delivery of their third tug to carry the name *Emperor*. Her managing owner, William John Thomas, was one of the foremost passenger steamer operators in Falmouth and in partnership with Albert Edward Benney, formed the River Fal Steamship Co Ltd. in 1906.

For those vessels described above as passenger-tugs, some evidence survives either to prove or reasonably suggest such use. Unfortunately it appears that passenger certification records held in some Marine Survey Offices of the Board of Trade are now destroyed when the vessels are broken up or otherwise disposed of. Some local authority passenger boat licensing records do survive however, and an interesting sample of the steamers' log books, from the Registrar General of Shipping and Seamen, which detail their annual trade, are deposited in the Cornwall Records Office. However, the demarcation between some of the vessels employed in the passenger and towage trades remains blurred. With only one exception, that being the *Jane*, all of the passenger steamers registered in the Ports of Falmouth and Truro between 1859 and 1883 were either tugs employed in the passenger trade or passenger steamers employed as tugs during the winter months.

During the first four years of the 1880s, there were at least twenty one tugs and passenger steamers working in the Ports of Falmouth and Truro. The following list of those vessels is not necessarily a complete survey of all such steamers operating in the district; it does not take into account any small undecked steamers of less than 15t.g., which would not have required registration. Neither are any vessels listed which might have been registered elsewhere.

Passenger steamers:

SS *Wotton* (1866)	St Mawes Ferry
SS *Jane* (1872)	St Mawes Ferry

Passenger-tugs:

SS *Emperor* (1882)	Excursions/towage
SS *Emperor* (1883)	Excursions/towage
SS *Victor* (1875)	Excursions/towage
SS *Resolute* (1877)	Excursions/towage
SS *New Resolute* (1882)	Excursions/towage

Tugs:

SS *Albert* (1879)
PS *Lady Bute* (1857)
SS *Briton* (1880)
SS *Pendragon* (1870)
SS *St Keverne* (1876)
SS *Laura* (1875)
SS *Carn Brea* (1882)
SS *Pendennis* (1881)
SS *Kimberley* (1878)

Other tugs included the *Falcon*, the *North Star*(1869) of Truro, and the *Triton*—forerunner of the well known local tug of the same name which was built by Cox & Co. in 1900 for the Falmouth Towage Company. There were two more tugs, the *Eagle* and the *Rosetta* of 1882, both of which held passenger certificates for the 1890 season. These two steamers could be 'engaged for excursions between Penzance and Start Point'. Separate cabins were available for Ladies and Gentlemen. The agents were J.H. Deeble & Sons, Engineers and Ships Chandlers (since 1860) of Arwenack Street, Falmouth. By the 1920s Deebles were also specialising in ships, commercial and domestic electrical engineering under the slogan 'Deebles way is the lightest way'.

The 52ft wooden screw tug *St Keverne*, listed above, also operated as a passenger steamer during 1890, with T. Hunkin as her Master and William Rowe of Killigrew Street as her agent. In addition to his professions of Auctioneer, Estate Agent, Emigration Agent and Shipping Agent, Rowe later owned two successive coastal passenger-tugs, both named *Penguin*.He was also the agent for, and later Chairman of, the St Mawes Steam Tug & Passenger Co. Ltd.

The tug *Kimberley*, named to commemorate the presentation of Kimberley Park to the people of Falmouth by the Earl of Kimberley in 1877, was owned by the Rusden family, of Falmouth. In 1884 they bought an 88 tons gross, 103' long, wood, screw tug, the *Armine*, which was built for them by Charles Burt of Falmouth and powered by a Sara & Burgess engine. The *Armine* was sold in 1890, but her name was revived by Charles Rusden in 1894 and given to his little passenger steamer on the Flushing Ferry. In 1896 Charles Rusden had built, at Dartmouth, the pleasure steamer *Truro Belle*.

William Henry Lean was a Falmouth shipbuilder and in addition to owning the 76·4ft long, wood, screw tug *Pendennis*, he also owned and managed his own trading vessels. In 1889 he built a wood, passenger, screw steamer, the *Falmouth Castle*, which was briefly employed by the Roseland & Falmouth Steam Packet Co Ltd. By the end of the century Lean's yard began building in steel.

Messrs. Pool, Skinner and Williams, builders of W.J. Thomas's passenger tug, the *Victor*, in 1898, and the foundry shipyard of Walter Cox, of the Bar, also specialised in iron and steel built ships. The origins of the Cox yard date back to the establishment of the family's ship chandlery business in the 1860s. Cox & Co. were responsible for the construction of each of the Fal's distinctive , tug-like, passenger steamers that survived in the district until 1939. Waterline drawings of the ten local passenger vessels constructed by Cox & Co. are reproduced in Appendix Two. The yard was also responsible for the construction of the well-remembered G.W.R. ferry steamer, *The Mew*, which plied between Kingswear Railway Station and Dartmouth. In addition, Cox & Co. built three paddle steamers for the River Dart Steamboat Co. Ltd. The compound diagonal engine from the first of these paddlers, built in 1904, survives in working order aboard the preserved River Dart paddle steamer, the *Kingswear Castle*. The Cox-built Dart paddler, *Compton Castle*, of 1914, today serves as a 'floating' restaurant, moored at Lemon Quay, Truro. Her engines are preserved by the Maritime Museum at Bembridge on the Isle of Wight. All of the yards noted above were located along the foreshore between Bar Road and Falmouth Docks.

From the 1890s, with only a few exceptions, the history of the Fal's towage trade follows a separate course. Although nearly all of the subsequent passenger steamers were built with a towing facility, they were built primarily as passenger carriers, maintaining a liberty to tow and/or seeking towage during the winter months, between November and April. Surviving some short lived competition and co-existing with a limited number of independent operators, the steamers associated with both the River Fal Steamship Co Ltd., and the St Mawes Steam Tug & Passenger Co Ltd., effectively divided the local passenger steamer trade between themselves and established a pattern of operation that was to survive until 1939.

Ruan Lanihorne Quay on the Ruan River. The Fal can be seen in the distance, with Lamorran Wood in the background. A plaque on the corner of the quay commemorates the presentation of the quay to the parishioners of Ruan Lanihorne by Mrs C Hyde in 1919. Barges traded to Ruan Lanihorne until the 1930s. There was a higher quay nearer to the village.
A K collection

W S Blamey's little passenger launch, the *Amy*, ran from Ruan Lanihorne (lower) quay to Truro on Wednesdays and Saturdays. She was converted to a steamer from one of the ss *Mohegan*'s ship's boats which survived the disastrous shipwreck of that liner in 1898. Mr Blamey stands amidships, beside the boiler.
Courtesy Peter Newman

The River Fal Steamship Co Ltd's steamer the *Princess Victoria* (on the left) heads downstream, while her fleet sister, the *New Resolute*, enters the Truro River. The course of the River Fal continues upstream to the right of Tregothnan House.

Photo: E A Bragg; A K collection

Messrs Handcock & Thomas' passenger tug, the *Emperor* moored off Tregothnan boathouse on a rare visit up river. Viscount Falmouth sometimes permitted church and philanthropic organisations to land at the boathouse for teas, laid out in the grounds.

A K collection

Truro, 1896. The passenger tug *New Resolute* is moored at Lemon Quay, adjacent to The Green, on the River Kenwyn. The building immediately behind the steamer's funnel is the Customs House. Astern is Town Quay. The Harbourmaster's Office, behind the quayside crane, remains today. The building on Town Quay itself was the premises of J Edwards, Agricultural Merchant & Traders (note the river barges alongside). This building was later replaced by the present structure, which itself was originally built for Coast Lines. In the foreground are the timber seasoning ponds and warehouses of Harveys. The River Allen is on the right. The main building of Truro Cathedral, in the background, was completed in 1900. By 1915 it had gained its spire. On the extreme right is the white building of the surviving Furniss Biscuit Factory.

Photo: E A Bragg; A K collection

The *New Resolute* at Town Quay c1906. The
steam launch unfortunately remains
unidentified, but would appear to have
been privately owned. The distinctive
topmast of a coastal trading ketch towers
above Edward's warehouse.

Falmouth Library

Worth's Quay in Truro was and still is, owned by the local authority. The pretty waiting shelter and iron railings fully enclosed the passenger landing. Entry to the quay was effected through turnstiles in the centre of the building. Unfortunately the shelter, which was built in 1911, was demolished in the 1960's when the A39 ring-road was built.

A K collection

River barges discharge at Town Quay whilst a healthy compliment of passengers embark aboard the *Princess Victoria* at Worth's Quay. The warehouses of Trafalgar Wharf and those backing off Malpas Road, tail away downstream.

A K collection

The *Resolute* moored off Malpas, with the cottages of Malpas Passage behind. A river lighter and a small vertical boilered steamer attend the topsail schooner on the right. Astern lies another schooner and in the distance a timber ship is attended by lighters and barges.

Royal Institution of Cornwall

The Malpas Ferry horseboat on the beach at Malpas Passage. The difficulty sometimes experienced in embarking a horse and cart, such as that depicted, might well be appreciated. At the shipyard of Scoble and Davies, in the background, a topsail schooner is careened for repairs and/or maintenance.

A K collection

The *New Resolute* approaching Malpas in 1912. On the shore, behind her bow, is the yard of Messrs Scoble and Davies where she was built. The passenger landing lies off the picture to the right.

Photo: H Hughes; Royal Institution of Cornwall

The *Princess Victoria* steams down the River Fal, passing Roundwood Quay. Coombe or Cowlands Creek stretches away behind the steamer. The mouth of Leemouth or Lamouth Creek is on the left. The one time mineral quay, then shipbuilding yard, was better known as the Plum Gardens to many late Victorian excursionists. The area surrounding both Coombe and the adjacent Church Creek is renowned for its Kea Plums.

Photo: E A Bragg; A K collection

Prior to the introduction of the steam ferry in 1889 carriages and wagons were transported across the King Harry Reach of the River Fal aboard this horseboat, similar to that employed at Malpas.
Photo: William Spreat; Stephen Rowson collection

The first steam powered King Harry Ferry, pictured on the Roseland, or Philleigh side of the river c1905. This chain ferry was built by Sara & Burgess Foundry at Penryn. She was equipped with a vertical boiler and a two cylinder compound engine driving two chain wheels. Some historians claim that the bridge was originally equipped with just one chain, but photographic evidence shows two chains fitted by 1897. The cogged chain wheels meshed with the submerged chain links to draw the ferry, or 'bridge', across the river.

The St Mawes Steam Tug & Passenger Co Ltd's excursion steamer, the *Alexandra*, heads upstream, *en route* either to Gatley's Quay on the Tresillian River or to turn on the Ruan River, near Tregothnan. The scene on the opposite Feock shore remains virtually unaltered today. The houses are owned by the ferry company to house the ferrymen and their families.
Falmouth Library

The paddle, passenger-tug *Pendennis* was closely associated with the Redruth & Chasewater Railway Company and their wharves at Devoran. She operated coastal excursions to Kynance Cove, Fowey and Plymouth, under the management of the Port of Falmouth Steam Tug Co Ltd. She later passed to successive owners on the East coast, at Peterborough, Wisbech, Lowestoft and Middlesborough, being broken up in 1923. She is pictured here in the Fenlands at Sutton Bridge on the River Nene, near Wisbech.

Richard Clammer collection

The Admiralty Dockyard in Mylor Creek.
The stone pier and some of the buildings
survive today as Mylor Yacht Harbour. In
the Churchyard on the right are buried
some of Flushing's Post Office Packet
Captains. The *Alexandra* steams down the
creek, having turned off Trelew Farm, a
little further upstream.

Photo: E A Bragg; A K collection

The motor launch *Ibis*. From a souvenir card
issued by P. Bell, her owner.
A K collection

The British & Irish Steam Packet Company's wooden paddler, the *Shannon*, maintained her Dublin-Falmouth-Plymouth-London route for twenty years until 1846. In December of that year she caught fire in Plymouth and was put ashore at Cattedown—as pictured in this Illustrated London News engraving. The fire blazed for about four hours, but was eventually brought under control. The *Shannon* later made her own way back to Dublin for repairs.

Royal Institution of Cornwall

Falmouth Harbour, c1870. A rather fanciful engraving viewing Pendennis Castle, the newly constructed docks and the Falmouth Hotel. The two paddlers depicted perhaps owe more to the artists imagination than reality, but three of the tugs known to be operating out of Falmouth at the time were indeed paddle steamers. They were Richard Taylor's *Sydney* and *Pendennis* (1863) and A Handcock's *Dandy* of 1863.

A K collection

Photographed from a similar viewpoint nearly fifty years later, this E A Bragg view shows the shipyard of Cox & Co on the Bar, just to the left of the Falmouth Hotel, which is in the centre of the picture. Cox & Co was later taken over by R & H Green and Silley Weir, becoming Silley, Cox & Co. In 1918 Silley, Cox & Co and the Falmouth Docks Co amalgamated to establish the engineering and ship repair dock that exists today. The Cox-built *Princess Victoria* steams towards the Prince of Wales Pier.

Photo: E A Bragg; A K collection

The *Wotton* ended her days at Belfast, where she is pictured with a Fleetwood–Belfast steamer in the background. She was finally broken up in the 1930s.

Roy Stribley collection

29

The *Emperor* of 1883 at Market Strand Quay,
Falmouth during the 1890's. Used almost
exclusively on coastal excursions, the
Emperor was active until the *Victor* took
over her trade in 1898. Owned by E A
Handcock and P Thomas, the *Emperor*
sports the distinctive Maltese Cross funnel
motif which was later adopted by W J
Thomas for the *Victor*.

Royal Institution of Cornwall

A rare photograph of the first two steamers of Benney & Co together at Market Strand Quay—the *New Resolute* and the *Resolute* (behind). The tiny tug astern of the *Resolute* is the *Lizard*, a boarding tug once owned by W Broad, the shipping agent. Eleven other tugs are moored in the harbour, their names infuriatingly indistinct!

P N Thomas collection

Passenger tugs could obviously be expected to engage in either the towage or excursion trades, but not usually at the same time! The *Princess Victoria* whilst *en route* with passengers, is pictured towing a three masted topsail schooner, thought to be the *Mary Barrow*, past Malpas.

The *Mary Barrow* was built by W H Lean at Falmouth in 1891. Originally registered in Barrow, she was later reregistered at Truro and worked out of Cornish ports. Her final skipper and part owner was Captain Peter Mortensen. In Basil Greenhill's *The Merchant Schooners*, a story is told that 'Mad' Peter Mortensen once put to sea in a gale because a crewman spat on the deck of the *Mary Barrow*. After the Second World War Peter Mortensen operated his motor cruiser, the *Viking*, out of St Mawes, with a licence for twelve passengers. His trippers hopefully refrained from fouling his deck, or they might have experienced a longer trip than anticipated.

Royal Institution of Cornwall

CHAPTER TWO

THE ST. MAWES STEAM TUG & PASSENGER CO LTD.
AND THE
FLUSHING FERRY

THE PERCUIL RIVER

On the eastern shore of the Carrick Roads, immediately before St Anthony Head and Falmouth Bay, lies St Mawes Harbour and the Percuil or Porthcuel River. The estuary takes its title from the small hamlet of Percuil which lies upon its eastern shoreline, about half way between St Mawes and the village of Gerrans. The name of the hamlet has been variously spelt over the years, with Percuil or Porthcuel predominating. I have adopted the former spelling, this being the one in general use for the greater part of the period covered by this book. Some guide books named the estuary the St Mawes River.

Two creeks, the Trethem and the short Polingey, each named after farms at their head, converge at an idyllic and isolated point above Percuil to form the main channel of the estuary. Being strategically positioned at a narrow point of this tidal barrier, between the communities of Gerrans and Portscatho to the east and the harbour of St Mawes to the west, Percuil long enjoyed some importance both as a landing place for Gerrans-bound cargoes and for its ferry across the Percuil River. The ferry met the Gerrans wagonette and attended the St Mawes steamers, which anchored offshore. Passengers from St Mawes were also conveyed across the river to visit the tea garden at Percuil. Unfortunately, steamer trips along this beautiful stretch of water are no longer available. The Percuil Ferry has also, long since, ceased running.

Across the estuary from St Mawes lies Place House and the church of St Anthony. A stone quay adjacent to the house served as a landing for steamer passengers and others from St Mawes who wished to visit the house and church, or walk to the lighthouse and coast at St Anthony Head, offering as it does spectacular views across Falmouth Bay and up the Carrick Roads. Until the 1970s these landings were still provided by A.S. Cook with his motor vessel, the *Evelina*. For many years he specialised in operating 'The Roseland Cruise', landing at Place House where morning coffee or afternoon teas were available.

The one-time fishing harbour of St Mawes has lost its original identity to a succession of villa, bungalow and holiday home developments, which have gradually transformed the community into the holiday village it has become today. It was undoubtedly the introduction of passenger steamers during the second half of the 19th century, linking St Mawes to the newly-arrived railway in Falmouth, which helped promote the transformation. The St Mawes ferryboats have continued to prosper from the trade for over a century. During the 1980s, four motor vessels, with a combined capacity for four hundred passengers, have worked the ferry. Ironically, the operators still describe St Mawes as a quaint Cornish fishing village. The substantial stone jetty at St Mawes protects the harbour from south westerly gales and provides a safe, sheltered landing for passenger boats. Modern motor vessels can land at low tide, even though only a few feet of water is available. The old steamer operators, however, made little or no concession for tidal conditions and continued to favour their deep draught, passenger-tug design. The St Mawes Steam Tug Passenger Co Ltd's *Alexandra* drew 6ft 3ins of water astern, about twice the depth available at St Mawes at low tide. Row boat tenders were pressed into service on such occasions.

THE WOTTON AND THE JANE

On 27th August, 1869, a group of St Mawes mariners, Ezekiel Tucker, William Jenking and Frederick Andrew, together with William Henry Williams, a merchant of London, purchased the iron, screw tug *Wotton* from Howard and Robert Fox, with the aim of establishing a passenger steamer service between St Mawes and Falmouth. The steamer measured 28·46t.g., 64 x 12·25 x 6·05ft and was powered by a simple two cylinder engine. Once converted for full-time passenger work she was granted certificates: no.5 (smooth water) for 167; no.4 (semi-smooth water) for 91; and no.3 (coastal excursion) for 66 passengers.. Prior to the *Wotton's* inauguration of this year-round, timetabled ferry, no such service existed. Passage could be obtained aboard the boats of local watermen, but were always subject to the elements on this exposed and sometimes rough crossing.

ST. MAWES STEAM TUG & PASSENGER Co.
LIMITED.

The Half-yearly General Meeting of the shareholders. of this Company will be held at the Company's Office, 2, Collet's Lane, St. Mawes, on *Monday August 5th*, 1872, at 7, p.m.

Question to be discussed—*Shall the " Wotton " be sold?*

HORATIO STEP.

The owners of the *Wotton* established the St Mawes Steam Tug & Passenger Co Ltd. in 1872. The steamer was initially sold to the new company, but later in the year reverted once again to the private ownership of the original shareholders. On 8th April 1878, Edward Handcock sold his 64 shares in the wood, screw steamer *Jane* to the St Mawes company. Included amongst the members of the St Mawes Steam Tug & Passenger Co.Ltd at this time were William Rowe of Falmouth and Edwin Hicks of St Mawes, both of whom were later to serve as Chairmen of the Company.

WILLIAM ROWE

William Rowe was the proprietor of Rowe & Sons, butchers, of Killigrew Street and Arwenack Street in Falmouth. Rowe also supplied meat and dairy produce to the Royal Navy and other shipping, from his own farm at Kegilliack, near Falmouth. It was from his premises at Killigrew Street that he acted as agent for the passenger-tug *St Keverne* in 1890. In addition to his interest in the St Mawes Steam Tug & Passenger Co.Ltd, William Rowe also established his own similarly named Falmouth Steam Towage & Passenger Company during the 1890s, to operate his seagoing passenger-tug, the *Penguin*. She was built by Cox & Co. and measured 104t.g., 90·6 x 18·3 x 9·7ft. In 1901 he took delivery of a replacement 187t.g. steel, passenger tug, also named the *Penguin* and also built by Cox & Co. She measured 120 x 21 x 12ft. Both vessels traded mainly as seagoing tugs in the home trade (i.e. in British coastal waters and to continental ports within the Elbe-Brest limits). They did however offer some excursions from Falmouth, steaming as far as Plymouth on occasions. Rowe was a partner in the shipping and estate agency business of Rowe & Liddicoat, but in 1902 he amalgamated with the similar business of H.J.R. Corlyon's, who was himself later to become the Secretary of the River Fal Steamship Co.Ltd. Collectively Messrs Rowe & Corlyon held agencies for the Castle Line to Africa, the Orient Line to Australia, the Allan and Dominion Lines to America and the Red Star, White Star and Cunard Lines to North America. During 1910, while William Rowe was the Chairman of the St Mawes Steam Tug & Passenger Co.Ltd, his son,

W.P. Hugo Rowe was appointed as the Company's Secretary, in succession to H. Clemon. Meanwhile in the same office of Rowe & Corlyon's in the Strand, Falmouth, H.J.R. Corlyon performed his duties as Secretary of the River Fal Steamship Co.Ltd. The benefit of this association is revealed in the virtual elimination of duplicated excursion programmes.

Following William Rowe's death in 1913, H.J.R.Corlyon established the auctioneering business of Corlyon & Sons in Market Street. He remained as Secretary of the River Fal Steamship Co.Ltd until its demise in 1942. W.P. Hugo Rowe went into partnership and established the business of Rowe & Knowles, estate agents, at the Strand office. From this office the affairs of the St Mawes Steam Tug & Passenger Co.Ltd continued to be managed until after the Second World War.

THE ROSELAND

When Ezekiel Tucker died in March 1889, his shares in the *Wotton* were purchased by Edwin Hicks of the St Mawes Steam Tug & Passenger Co.Ltd. However, the steamer continued in the private ownership of Hicks and William Jenking for another seven years. William Jenking's son, Edward, of Roseland Cottage, St Mawes, subsequently became Master of the Company's excursion steamer, the *Alexandra* and in 1917 was additionally appointed as Managing Owner of all the Company's vessels. Edwin Hicks became Chairman of the Company, succeeded by his son, Edwin David Hicks, who in 1936 additionally took over as Managing Owner of the Company's steamers.

Early in 1886 the St Mawes Steam Tug & Passenger Co.Ltd took delivery of a new steel, screw, passenger steamer. Built by Cox & Co she measured 41t.g., 72·9 x 13·5 x 6·7ft and was equipped with triple expansion engines built at Cox & Co's foundry. Named the *Roseland*, this steamer was to serve almost exclusively on the St Mawes ferry for fifty years. The new steamer closely resembled the *Wotton* in appearance, but was completed with two small below-deck saloons. The forward saloon, no more than twelve feet in length, was a rather spartan affair, providing only basic shelter from inclement crossings. But the even smaller after saloon was fitted with comfortable upholstered seating. The ladies toilet was located off this saloon. In later years a little deckhouse was built above the after 'ladies' saloon and was unofficially and rather irreverently referred to as 'the cowshed'. William Jenking was appointed as the first Master of the *Roseland*.

During the same year that the *Roseland* was launched, the foundry of James Hill of Gerrans supplied a new two cylinder engine for the *Jane*. The steamer was then withdrawn from passenger service and converted for trawling. On May 1st 1888 she was stranded in Port Eynon Bay, South Wales, in a south westerly gale. In his book, *Westcountry Passenger Steamers*, Graham Farr records that her crew of two were saved by two men wading out from the shore with a rope. The *Jane* was salvaged but sold on 26th October of the same year to John Rowlands, an innkeeper from nearby Swansea.

THE ROSELAND AND FALMOUTH STEAM PACKET CO.LTD

The St Mawes Steam Tug & Passenger Co.Ltd faced serious competition during the last years of the 1880s. The Roseland & Falmouth Steam Packet Co Ltd. was incorporated in 1887 to operate a steamer service between St Mawes and Falmouth. The promoter and manager of the Company, and master of the Company's first steamer, the *St Mawes Castle*, was Richard Samuel Collins of Albert Terrace, St-Mawes. His iron, screw steamer measured 48t.g., 75·0 x 15·1 x 6·3ft and was built by Harvey's of Hayle*. After one year in service the *St Mawes Castle* was lengthened by seven feet at W.H. Lean's Falmouth yard. The reason for the alteration remains obscure, but that considerable expense was incurred is indicated by an advertisement placed by the Roseland & Falmouth Steam Packet Co.Ltd in the *Falmouth Packet* newspaper during July 1888. It noted the 'improvement' and added 'A few shares to meet the expense of alterations are offered to the public, 5 shillings to be paid on application and 5

---

* The history of steamship building at the foundry shipyard of Harvey's of Hayle dates back to 1831. The Hayle company specialised in building shallow river steam boats, tugs and steam barges and was responsible for a number of passenger steamers which operated on the rivers and estuaries of South Devon.

shillings within one month of allotment'. It can only be presumed that such drastic remedial action became necessary either to counter instability or to cure some other disastrous characteristic.

William Henry Lean built a 24t.g., wood, screw, passenger steamer in 1889. She measured 55·8 x 13·2 x 5·8ft and was fitted with a compound inverted engine, manufactured in Lean's own foundry six years earlier. During 1889 the steamer entered service for the Roseland & Falmouth Steam Packet Co.Ltd, and was named the *Falmouth Castle*.

In 1891 an offer was made and accepted for both of the Company's steamers, by the Ship Canal Passenger Steamer Syndicate Ltd of Manchester, who were acquiring passenger steamers in anticipation of the completion of the Manchester Ship Canal. The Roseland & Falmouth Steam Packet Co.Ltd was subsequently dissolved. In 1895 both steamers were transferred to the Ship Canal Passenger Steamer Co (1893) Ltd. The *St Mawes Castle* was resold in 1897 to the West Australian Steam Packet Company, but foundered *en route* to Australia, in the Indian Ocean.

ROYAL MAIL STEAMERS

Prior to the advent of motor transport, the most convenient route for the mail of the Roseland Peninsula was via Falmouth's branch line railway and by steamer to St Mawes and Percuil. The resulting Royal Mail contract won by the St Mawes Steam Tug & Passenger Co.Ltd therefore subsidised the year round steamer service and provided the Company with the opportunity of applying the prestigious R.M.S. prefix to their steamers. The times of the St Mawes Ferry varied over the years and even altered from winter to summer, but the twice daily mail runs remained virtually constant. The timetable detailed below was in operation during April 1900 and serves to illustrate the daily working pattern (Sunday's excepted) followed by the *Roseland* for fifty years.

The steamer departed from St Mawes for the first crossing of the day at 7.00AM The return from Falmouth at 7.40AM was made with the incoming mail on board. On this trip calls were made at St Mawes, St Anthony (Place House) and Percuil. The Gerrans district outgoing mail was embarked at Percuil and the steamer left for St Mawes at 9.00AM. From St Mawes the steamer departed for Falmouth at 9.30AM. The second trip of the day called at St Mawes, St Anthony and Percuil. At Percuil, on this second run, the steamer was met by the morning wagonette from Gerrans and Portscatho. Another crossing was made departing from Percuil at 11.15AM and St Mawes at 11.45AM. The first afternoon ferry from Falmouth left at 1.00PM, calling at St Mawes only. The second mail run followed, where the steamer additionally met the afternoon wagonette from Gerrans and Portscatho. The return mail run departed from Percuil at 3.35PM and St Mawes at 4.00PM. One more trip calling at all the landings left Falmouth at 5.30PM. The day ended with two return trips between St Mawes and Falmouth, the last crossing from Falmouth being at 9.00PM. The return fare between Falmouth and any landing on the Percuil River was 6d.

EXCURSION STEAMERS

The St Mawes Steam Tug & Passenger Co.Ltd took delivery of a new 66t.g. steel, screw steamer in April 1894. She was built by Cox & Co. and was named *Princess May*. The steamer measured 76·9 x 16·6 x 6·9ft and was powered by a triple expansion engine, also built by Cox. The *Princess May* offered two below-deck saloons with her after deck seating carried on a raised poop deck, giving greater headroom to the after 'Ladies' saloon. The steamer immediately embarked upon a full excursion programme. Coastal trips to the Helford River and the Lizard Peninsula were offered. She visited Portscatho, Portloe and rounded the Dodman Point to call at Mevagissey. The *Princess May* also steamed up the Carrick Roads to visit Mylor and Restronguet Creeks and the Ruan and Tresillian Rivers. Most of the Company's excursions commenced from St Mawes and/ or Percuil, calling at Falmouth *en route*. The excursion boat thus provided additional ferry crossings, which during the peak summer season released the *Roseland* to provide occasional short excursions to St Just in Roseland, where passengers could land for one hour.

On 12th March 1896 the *Wotton* finally surrendered

her independence, when William Jenking and Edward Hicks sold their shares to the St Mawes Steam Tug & Passenger Co Ltd. The *Wotton* was almost immediately resold to William Henry Lean and in May 1897 was again sold by him to James Watkins, the London tug owner.

After just eight years in the St Mawes company's ownership, the *Princess May* was sold back to Cox & Co. in February 1902. Walter Resleigh Cox of the shipbuilding company had learned of a good price being offered for just such a general purpose vessel by the Port Elizabeth Harbour Board in South Africa. He immediately resold the *Princess May* to Port Elizabeth, where she arrived during the following May. A replacement steamer was laid down at Cox's yard and delivered in December of the same year. One can only presume that the deal proved profitable for the St Mawes company's shareholders, as the company endured the entire summer season without an excursion steamer.

The replacement for the *Princess May* was a 73t.g., steel, screw steamer named the *Alexandra*. She measured 84·6 x 16·9 x 7·7ft, with lines that made little or no concession to her design as a tug. Under similar circumstances to those surrounding the sale of the *Princess May*, Walter Cox had previously resold the Cox-built, Truro registered, passenger steamer *Victoria* in 1900, after just one season on the Fal. The overtly tug-like design of the *Alexandra* might therefore indicate the anticipation of a similar deal. In the event, however, the *Alexandra* was to remain with the St Mawes company until she was acquired by the Ministry of War Transport in 1916. She was subsequently sold as a tug in 1919 to W.J. Reynolds of Torpoint, on the River Tamar.

The *Alexandra* held class 4 and class 3 passenger certificates, enabling her to provide both river and coastal excursions. Her class 4 certificate permitted trips to the Helford River, across Falmouth Bay. Coastal excursions on her class 3 certificate however, required the services of a certificated skipper and a certificated engineer. Reproduced in Appendix Three are details from the 'official log books and accounts of voyages and crew' of the two river/coastal steamers, the *Alexandra* and the *Queen of the Fal*, for 1913. The complete programme of excursions for all of the steamers operating from Falmouth Harbour during the week Monday 18th–Saturday 23rd August, 1913, is also reproduced in Appendix Four.

Following acquisition by the Ministry of War Transport of the *Alexandra* in 1916, the St Mawes Steam Tug & Passenger Co.Ltd was granted permission by the Ministry to order a replacement vessel from the yard of Silley, Cox & Co. Entered in the Falmouth Register of Shipping as Port No.1 of 1917, the new steamer was named the *St Mawes*. Whilst retaining the design elements of a tug, the St Mawes was first and foremost a passenger steamer. She offered the usual two below deck saloons and additionally boasted a deck shelter and an upper deck. She measured 80t.g., 75·6 x 18·0 x 7·6ft and was equipped with a triple expansion engine driving a single screw, which gave a trials speed of 9·5 knots. The *St Mawes* was to be the last steam vessel built for the Company. Upon completion in June 1917, the *St-Mawes* was immediately hired by the Ministry of War Transport for harbour service. She entered public service for the first time in 1920.

MOTOR VESSELS

Throughout the country during the late 1920s there was an acceleration in the introduction of passenger motor vessels. A combination of circumstances, including rising coal prices after the miners and General Strike, and the proliferation of motor bus and charabanc services, altered the nature of the estuarine passenger boat trade. On the Fal these changes proceeded at a conservative pace, indeed, until the middle of the 1930s only one passenger motor vessel was introduced. The steel, motor vessel *St Gerrans* was built by Silley, Cox & Co. in 1927. She measured 73t.g., 69·25 x 17·35 x 5·5ft, and was powered by Gardiner Semi Diesel engines. Whether a compressed air or a hot bulb system was employed to ignite these early Diesel and Semi Diesel engines, each possessed its own idiosyncrasies known intimately to its regular engineer. Thus when the *St-Gerrans* was requisitioned for war service at Devonport during the Second World War, she would not even start without the understanding attention of her Falmouth engineer, who was hurriedly sent for. In a district where the basic design concept of a passenger steamer had changed little in a lifetime, the *St Gerrans* was revolutionary and caused quite a stir locally when she entered service in 1927. She was licensed for 280 passengers within Falmouth Harbour and 168 for coastal trips within the limits of Black Head and Dodman Point, thus excluding any Lizard or Mevagissey trips.

The fleet of three vessels, SS *Roseland*, SS *St Mawes* and MV *St Gerrans* were joined during the 1930s by a small, unregistered, wooden, motor launch, the *Berry Castle*. During this period the *St Gerrans* could usually be found performing the St Mawes mail runs and on trips to the Helford River. The *St Mawes* was also regularly rostered on the St-Mawes ferry and was additionally employed to operate the Company's only remaining coastal trips to Porthoustock and Portscatho. Both the *Roseland* and the *Berry Castle* were used almost exclusively on the St Mawes ferry.

In 1938, over fifty years from the date that the *Roseland* was originally introduced, the St Mawes Steam Tug & Passenger Co Ltd sought a suitable replacement for their ageing steamer. The Company bought a 59 t.g., steel, motor vessel, the *Royal Jubilee*. She was built in 1935 by Cook, Welton & Gemell Ltd, of Beverley, near Hull. Measuring 69·6 x 17·1 x 5·4ft, she was powered by a four stroke engine supplied by the Berguis Company of Glasgow. For three years the *Royal Jubilee* had operated cruises out of Bridlington. The motor vessel was registered in Falmouth in 1938, suitably renamed the *New Roseland*. Whatever the intended role awaiting the *Roseland*, world events were soon to determine both hers and the *St Mawes* immediate futures.

The declaration of war in September 1939 drew to a close the history of steam powered passenger vessels on the waters of the Fal estuary. The *St Mawes* was immediately hired on examination service and in August 1942 was purchased by the Ministry of War Transport for service on the Clyde. After the war, on 10th August 1947, her Falmouth registry was closed and transferred to Inverness, where the steamer was broken up just three years later. The *St Gerrans* was requisitioned for use at Devonport, but following the difficulty experienced with her temperamental engines, she was exchanged for the *New Roseland*. The *New Roseland* served as a barrage balloon vessel in the Bristol Channel. The *Roseland* remained in local waters but after the war she was sold to the Falmouth Docks & Engineering Co Ltd., for use as a workboat. The steamer was later utilised as a committee boat by Flushing Sailing Club. Well into the 1950s the outline of a steamer could be detected in Ponsharden Creek, between Penryn and Falmouth. Here the *Roseland* ended her days, as a houseboat, surviving as the last example of a Cox built, Falmouth Harbour, passenger-tug, a series of steamers of which she had also been the first.

THE FLUSHING FERRY

Water transport between the village of Flushing and Falmouth, on the Penryn River, still remains as the most expeditious method of gaining the opposite shore. Waterborne travellers will have completed their passage to Falmouth long before the motor car passenger has even joined the queue at the traffic lights in Penryn.

Included amongst the series of rewards bestowed by Charles II upon his Royalist allies in Cornwall, was the Flushing Ferry, the rights of which he granted to Sir Peter Killigrew in 1660. Over the centuries the Ferry was leased to successive ferrymen and in 1877, John Mead of Greenbank took over the operation. One or two open boats were used, being either rowed or sailed between Flushing Quay and Greenbank Quay. In August 1888 Mead purchased a steamboat, the *Greyhound*, from the Oreston & Turnchapel Steamboat Co Ltd. of the River Plym. The *Greyhound* measured 48·5 x 11·4 x 4·6ft and was a wooden, screw steamer of 16 t.g. She was built by F. Darton of Turnchapel at a date prior to 1869. Her engine is listed in the Falmouth register as two cylinder, built by Sara of Penryn. Throughout their history, the Oreston & Turnchapel Steamboat Co Ltd. bought and sold boats and engines as separate units. As the *Greyhound* cost John Mead just £111, it is likely that she arrived without an engine, and that the Sara unit was a local addition, just possibly the old engine from Benney's *Resolute*, which had received a new Cox built unit two years previously. Following the introduction of the *Greyhound*, the Falmouth landing was moved to Market Strand Quay, nearer the town centre. Local watermen took over the shorter crossing of the old Greenbank route. A table of watermens fares for the five stations and three districts within the Port of Falmouth is reproduced on the inside back cover.

By 1894 the lease of the Ferry seems to have passed to Charles Rusden, an engineer, of Garth House, Falmouth. In that year the *Greyhound* was joined by a second, smaller steamer. She was a 7·3t.g. launch, built by White of Cowes in 1886. The little steamer measured 37·8 x 9·0 x 4·3ft and since 1893 was powered by a two cylinder engine, built by Plenty of Newbury. Purchased secondhand by Rusden, she was named the *Armine*, after his family's earlier 87·4t.g. tug. During the following year Rusden took delivery of a new steamer, which not only differed dramatically from the *Armine*, but differed considerably from any contemporary passenger vessel on the Fal. The new steamer was built in Dartmouth in July 1895. She was a steel, screw steamer measuring 28·46t.g., 64·9 x 15·0 x 3·6ft. Her compound inverted, direct acting engine was supplied by Enock Bros. of Coombe Works, Dartmouth, but it remains unclear whether the vessel was also built by Enock Bros. or in the nearby Sandquay Yard of Philip's. Charles Rusden, the sole shareholder, registered her in the Port of Truro as the *Truro Belle*, on 9th July 1895. The *Truro Belle* differed from all other passenger steamers on the Fal in that she was built purely as an excursion steamer, with no towage facility. Unfortunately the duration of this attractive steamer's career on the Fal, under Rusden's command, was very brief. Within three years she was sold off the river to Capt. Coulson Douglas of Sunderland, for the Elswick & Dunston Ferry Company of Newcastle. In 1904 she was sold once again and worked briefly on the Forth & Clyde Canal. In January 1897 the *Armine* was sold. Initially purchased by William Langrish Russel, a Weymouth sailmaker, the *Armine* passed to the ownership of the Great Western Railway Company in 1899. The railway company used her as a harbour craft at Weymouth until January 1936. She was then sold once again and reportedly converted to a motor vessel for private use.

So drew to a close Charles Rusden's brief flirtation with the Fal's passenger steamer trade. The *Greyhound* survived in the district until broken up in 1904. At around 1900 her place on the Flushing Ferry was taken by another small, screw steamer, the *Lily*. Little information has come to light concerning this vessel, but fortunately she was captured for posterity in a photograph of Market Strand Quay, taken in 1901 (see page 53). The Ferry lease passed to Jack Angel and in 1901 he bought another steamer from the Oreston & Turnchapel Steamboat Co.Ltd. Named the *Express*, she had been launched from Darton's Mt. Batten boatyard in 1881. Her engines were built by the expatriate Cornish engineering and foundry company of Tangye of Birmingham. Whilst at Plymouth the ferry boat was licenced to carry 110 passengers. The River Plym company retubed her boiler in 1901 and sold her to Jack Angel for £300. It is possible that the *Express* survived the First World War, having passed, along with the Ferry lease, to the ownership of Charles Hughes in 1913. However, the ageing steamer was either joined or replaced by a new motor vessel, the *Miranda*, in 1914, introducing the nomenclature that is synonymous with the Flushing Ferry to this day. The Falmouth Guide for 1914 notes '. . . . . .that a new and conveniently fitted motor boat of ample capacity has been inaugurated for passenger traffic from the Prince of Wales Pier at Falmouth to and from Flushing at regular times throughout the day excepting Sundays'. The Guide also notes that the Mylor Bridge wagonette provided four trips each way to link with the Flushing Ferry on Tuesdays and Saturdays at 3d. each way.

During the mid-1920s, Horace Reece of Flushing operated the Ferry, succeeded in 1933 by Robert Arthur Kessel, a boat builder of Trefusis Street, Flushing. Kessel immediately set about building a sister vessel to the *Miranda* and in 1934 launched the similar-looking, 36ft long, motor vessel, the *Miranda II*.

Trethem Creek winds away into the distance on the left. A quay located half way up Polingey Creek, on the right, served Polingey Farm which can be seen standing amidst a group of trees near the bottom of the hill. The land which provided the viewpoint for this photograph is owned by the National Trust.

Photo: A K

The small group of buildings on the left of the photograph constitute the hamlet of Percuil. Sadly none of these cottages remain, having all been demolished after the Second World War owing to their poor condition. In retrospect perhaps their ruins would have been preferable to the structure which now occupies the site, built to serve the yachting community.

On the beach at Percuil, the passenger steamer *Alexendra* can be seen careened, that is beached and brought to lie on one side for the purpose of maintenance or cleaning and painting the hull. The St Mawes ferry steamer *Roseland* is departing for St Mawes. The shallow inlet behind the *Roseland* is named Pelyn Creek.

Photo: E A Bragg; A K collection

Place House viewed from Polvarth Point, St Mawes, before the open fields in the foreground were developed amid the sprawl of the modern 'resort'. The steamer landing at Place was adjacent to the house, on the left but hidden from view in this photograph. As the *Roseland* approaches St Mawes from Percuil, she is passing a pilot cutter, a fishing boat and other small craft moored offshore in the Percuil River.

Photo: E A Bragg; A K collection

On the Ordnance Survey map a public footpath is shown leading down this slipway and continuing across the water! This is the landing at Place, with St Mawes in the distance. At low tide this inlet virtually empties and is fordable. Only a shallow ribbon of water remains, near the eastern shoreline, leading to the slip. A boatyard once thrived at Cellars Beach, on the shore immediately opposite the slipway. The yard built pilot cutters, fishing boats, quay punts and other small craft.

Photo: A K

Passengers landing by a small boat from a steamer, at low tide in St Mawes Harbour. The quayside building on the extreme right bears a nameboard proclaiming it the 'Steamer Office & Waiting Room'.

A K collection

Market Strand Quay, c1890. From left to right, the steamers are the *New Resolute*, the *Wotton* and manoeuvering off the quay, a steamer believed to be the Roseland & Falmouth Steam Packet Company's *St Mawes Castle*.

Falmouth Library

William Rowe's second sea going tug to bear the name *Penguin*. She was built by Cox & Co in 1901 and worked as a tug in the Home Trade. Occasional coastal excursions from Falmouth were offered aboard the steamer. She was sold in 1905 to the Societé Dunquerquoise de Remorg de Suir..

Roy Stribley collection

A portrait of the *Roseland*, photographed off St Mawes Quay, c1905, by E A Bragg of Falmouth. A sign in the field behind advertises 'For Sale-Freehold Building Land'.

Photo: E A Bragg; A K collection

The *Roseland* at Percuil, c1920. Note the landing stage, which could be moved up and down the shore with the tide.
Photo: Osbornes, Falmouth

The *Roseland*, complete with her after deckhouse, mooring at St Mawes in the 1930s.
Photo: Hawke of Helston; A K collection

Benney & Co's *New Resolute* moored at Market Strand Quay, with the *Princess May* alongside. The St Mawes steamer bears a Royal Mail headboard on the front of her wheelhouse.

Royal Institution of Cornwall

Few pictures seem to have survived of the *Princes May* during her relatively short stay on the Fal. Her distinctive raised afterdeck is evident in this photograph, taken c1900. In common with Benney & Co's *Queen of the Fal*, the steel bulwarks of the after saloon were almost concealed, appearing to be a continuation of the black painted gunwhales which line the remaining deck.

Roy Stribley collection

The *Alexandra* at St Mawes Quay, c1905.
Photo: E A Bragg; A K collection

The Prince of Wales Pier in 1913. The *Alexandra* is in the foreground, with the *New Resolute* and the *Roseland* behind. On the far side of the pier is the *Queen of the Fal* (2). Two delivery carts are on the pier, one of them from the G.W.R. station on the other side of Falmouth.

Photo: E A Bragg; A K collection

After the First World War the *Alexandra* was sold to W J Reynolds of Torpoint, on the River Tamar. She is pictured off Torpoint, having been converted for towage work only.

Roy Stribley collection

The *St Mawes* moored in an unusual location, off the King Harry Ferry landing, near Feock. She would appear to be engaged upon a charter trip, c1930. The King Harry Ferry No 2 is pictured crossing the river. Built by Cox & Co in 1913, this ferry survived until 1950.

Roy Stribley collection

At low tide the *St Mawes* moored off St Mawes Quay and embarked and disembarked her passengers by small boats. To help achieve maximum pulling power a tug's propeller should be immersed as deeply in the water, and be as large as the draught permits. The three excursion steamers of the St Mawes Steam Tug & Passenger Co Ltd, the *Alexandra*, *Princess May* and the *St Mawes*, each forfeited the necessary shallow draught required to work to St Mawes at low tide, in favour of maintaining an effective towing capability. This photograph of the *St Mawes* is thought to show the steamer in 1920, her first season in public service, having been employed by the government since she was built in 1917.

Photo: Osbornes of Falmouth

The motor vessel *St Gerrans* in St Mawes Harbour.

A K collection

A degree of mystery surrounds the St Mawes Steam Tug & Passenger Co Ltd's small motor launch, the *Berry Castle*. Steamer historians—this author included—have maintained that the *Berry Castle* was chartered from the River Dart Steamboat Co Ltd during the 1930s. However, both local opinion and some photographic evidence suggest that the boat pictured here was *Berry Castle*, which was owned by the St Mawes company. Whilst there is no question that this vessel and the River Dart boat are indeed different launches, it remains unclear why the St Mawes boat would have been named after a castle near Totnes, on the River Dart! *Berry Castle* is moored off Place, at low tide, while her skipper rows the tender to pick up passengers waiting on the shore.

A K collection

The *New Roseland* first entered service at Falmouth in 1938, and so pre-war photographs are therefore thin on the ground. She is seen here at St Mawes Quay during the late 1950s.

A K collection

The *Roseland*, first of the Cox built passenger tugs, in use as a houseboat in Ponsharden Creek, c1950.
Roy Stribley collection

The Flushing Ferry steamer *Greyhound* approaching Market Strand Quay, c1890, with the village of Flushing in the background.
Royal Institution of Cornwall

Charles Rusden's excursion steamer, the *Truro Belle*, passing the Feock landing place of the King Harry Ferry. Elements of *Truro Belle*'s design were reflected in other contemporary Dartmouth built screw- and paddle-steamers, to be found on the River Dart, River Tamar and the Kingsbridge Estuary. Steam launches, passenger craft and tugs were built in Dartmouth by Enock Bros. (later W Ball) of Coombe Works, Philip & Son at Sandquay and at Simpson & Strickland's Noss Works which is currently occupied by Philip & Son Ltd.

Royal Institution of Cornwall

The *Truro Belle* steaming upstream towards Truro. Rusden's steamer endured a varied but brief career. After a spell on the Tyne, the *Truro Belle* moved even further north to the Forth & Clyde Canal, where James Main, a Glasgow shipowner, put her into competition with James Aitken's popular 'Queen' steamers. The Fal steamer was withdrawn before the end of the season and mortgaged to the Bank of Scotland. She was sold to a Dundee owner in 1905 and scrapped in 1907.

Royal Institution of Cornwall

It is indeed fortunate that this photograph was taken, showing as it does a collection of relatively rarely photographed steamers together at Market Strand Quay in 1901. Nearest the camera is the little Flushing Ferry steamer, the *Lily*. Next is the *Roseland*, with William Rowe's first *Penguin* moored alongside. The steamer on the far side of the quay, with the Maltese Cross funnel motif is the *Emperor* of 1883. The River Fal Steamship Company's *Victoria* can just be distinguished at the back. Also seen, on the left of the picture, is the stern of a sixth steamer, probably Benney & Co's *Queen of the Fal*.

Photo: Osbornes of Falmouth

Jack Angel's Flushing Ferry steamer, the *Express*, passing the old ferry landing at Greenbank, on the right.

Photo: Osbornes of Falmouth

THE FALMOUTH-FLUSHING CUNARDER.
HH 408

The first motor vessel on the Flushing Ferry, the *Miranda*, was built in 1914 and is pictured here during the early 1920s. The allusion to Cunard might possibly reflect the shipping company's move in 1919, from Liverpool to Southampton. Cunard liners calling in at Plymouth with the mails would have passed within sight of Falmouth.

A K collection

CHAPTER THREE
THE RIVER FAL STEAMSHIP CO LTD.

WILLIAM JOHN THOMAS

THE VICTOR

The tug owning ventures of Philip Thomas, from the *Dolphin* of 1866 through to the *Emperor* of 1883, were traced in the first chapter. During the 1890s his shipping interests passed to his son, William John Thomas. The first passenger vessel in which W.J. Thomas seems to have held a personal interest was the *Victor* of 1898. Her name might have originated from the Thomas family's business associations with the Handcocks. E.A. Handcock once held shares in the *Victor* of 1875. Indeed, the tugs *Victor*(1), *Emperor*(1) – owned by P. Thomas, *Emperor*(2) – owned in partnership by E.A. Handcock and P. Thomas, and *Victor*(2) of 1898, would appear to have succeeded each other in the coastal towage and excursion trades. The *Victor* of 1898 was built of steel by Messrs Pool, Skinner & Williams of The Bar, Falmouth. She measured 153t.g., 106 x 20 x 11·3ft. Triple expansion engines were supplied from the neighbouring foundry of Cox & Co. Shares in the steamer changed hands regularly, but the majority, if not all, passed amongst members of the Thomas family. Mrs Caroline Thomas, Philip Thomas' widow, was designated as Managing Owner until the tug was requisitioned by the Admiralty during the First World War. W.J. Thomas officially assumed control upon the steamer's return in 1919. In practice however it was he who managed the daily affairs of the steamer, from the day her keel was laid, until his death in 1934.

Giving up his career as a deep sea sailor following a shipwreck in the South China Sea, Frederick Martin of Falmouth oversaw construction of the *Victor* for W.J. Thomas. Upon completion of the passenger tug, Martin was appointed as Engineer, a post he was to fill until 1933, just one year before the steamer's long career at Falmouth drew to a close. The *Victor*'s name became synonymous with both local and longer distance coastal excursions out of Falmouth. She rarely plied upon the Fal above St Just Pool. The *Victor* survived to be the last true passenger-tug in the district, her comfortable after saloon being closed up at the end of each excursion season, while her crew sought winter work in the local coastal and salvage tug trades. Only a few months after the *Victor* entered service, the liner *Mohegan*, *en route* between Tilbury and New York, struck the Manacle Rocks, off Porthoustock on the Lizard coast. The *Victor* numbered amongst the rescue and salvage vessels that immediately steamed out from Falmouth to assist. The *Mohegan* sank within ten minutes with a loss of 106 lives. Six months later, on May 20th 1889, the *Victor*, in company with the Falmouth tug *Dragon*, raced out once again to the assistance of another transatlantic liner. This time the *Paris* had run aground at Lowland Point, Coverack. Both the *Victor* and the *Dragon* ferried the compliment of 300 passengers safely ashore at Falmouth. Two months later, on July 12th, the *Victor*, assisted in refloating the liner, having in the interim earned a healthy income by offering sightseeing excursions from Falmouth to view the stranded ship. The *Victor*, the *Dragon* and the *Triton* of 1900 were called out for salvage work along the immediate Cornish coastline on many other occasions. Both the *Victor* and the *Triton* deputised for short periods on the Isles of Scilly packet run from Penzance. The *Victor*'s regular programme of excursions along the Lizard coast offered landings at Porthoustock, Coverack and Church Cove (Landewednack). These trips were augmented with longer excursions to visit Mevagissey, Fowey and occasionally Plymouth.

During the First World War the passenger-tug was employed by the Admiralty and renamed the *Ictor* for the duration. On her return to public service at Falmouth in 1920, the most noticeable change was the absence of her distinctive, cast iron Maltese Cross funnel motif. Mr H. Leslie Martin, grandson of the *Victor*'s engineer, threw some light on the fate of one of these castings when he recalled a big Maltese Cross which, during the 1920s and 1930s, adorned the gate of his grandfather's house, off Trelawney Road. The *Victor* continued to offer coastal excursions until, in 1933, Frederick Martin decided to retire. During the following year W.J. Thomas died and the remaining family shareholders sold the steamer to Mrs Jennet Dewsbury of Swansea, in November 1934. The *Victor* was hired by the Ministry of War Transport in October 1939, being used initially on examination service and between 1942 and 1945 as a harbour tug on the Clyde. It was there that Frederick Martin's grandson saw her for the last time. Recognising her outline, but seeing no name, Mr Martin boarded the tug, satisfying himself that it was indeed the *Victor* when he discovered the engine builder's plate, bearing the legend: 'Cox & Co., Engineers & Shipbuilders, Falmouth, England'.

The *Victor* was never directly connected with any other passenger steamship company in Falmouth, remaining in the separate ownership of shareholders drawn from the Thomas family. As one of the founders of the River Fal Steamship Co Ltd., in 1906, it might safely be presumed that W.J. Thomas so arranged the *Victor*'s excursion programme to ensure the elimination of any competition with his other passenger steamer interests.

THE VICTORIA (1900)

To augment the *Victor*'s coastal excursion programme, with river trips on the Fal itself, William Thomas, in partnership with Arthur William Chard, ordered a second passenger steamer in 1899. Thomas' partnership with A.W. Chard, a gentleman who later served as a J.P. and Mayor of Falmouth, extended to the business of Chard & Thomas (ex Chard & Sons), General & Coal Merchants of Customs House Quay, Fish Strand and Bar Yard. Partnership with a coal merchant reaped obvious benefits and Chard's 32 shares in the new steamer ensured his vested interest. The partners adopted the title, the River Fal Steamship Company.

Completed by Cox & Co. in May 1900, the new twin screw, steel steamer measured 67·74t.g., 82 x 17·4 x 6·7ft. Inverted compound engines were supplied from the Cox foundry. Named the *Victoria*, she was entered into the Truro register as Port No.1 of 1900, and Capt. George Stoddern was appointed as Master. From June, the steamer provided a regular service between Falmouth and Malpas or Truro, depending upon the state of the tide. Just six months later, on 26th November, the *Victoria* was sold to Walter Resleigh Cox. Her registry was closed and transferred to Port Louis, Mauritius. The steamer had fallen victim to the Falmouth tradition, one particularly favoured by the Thomas family, of selling available tonnage to a ready buyer and replacing with a new, usually similar vessel. This time Walter Cox promised to have a replacement ready for the commencement of the following season.

THE VICTORIA (1901)

Completed in June 1901 and registered in Truro, the new steamer was immediately employed in 'towing and carrying passengers in the harbour only'. Inevitably named the *Victoria*, the twin screw steamer closely resembled her predecessor, measuring 67·82t.g., 85 x 18·1 x 6·4ft. She was painted in the same attractive livery with a white hull and buff funnel. The most obvious difference in her appearance was the provision of an upper deck and a deck shelter. A.W. Chard and W.J. Thomas remained as partners in the River Fal Steamship Company and initially as equal share holders in the new passenger tug. But within a month interest in the vessel was sold to various additional shareholders, included amongst whom were William Chellew and his son, Richard Berryman Chellew. For a number of years William Chellew, of Point, near Devoran, had worked sail trading vessels out of Devoran and Truro. During the 1880s Chellew established the Cornwall Steamship Company and introduced the tramp steamers, *City of Truro* and the *Duke of Cornwall*, amongst others. As regular visitors to the South Wales coal ports, the company had long maintained an office in Cardiff. It would seem likely that the Chard & Thomas coal which fired the *Victor* and *Victoria*, had arrived at Falmouth in the holds of Chellew's ships.*. W.J. Thomas was designated as Managing Owner of the *Victoria* and Capt. George Stoddern of Devonshire Place, Falmouth, took command. The steamer plied almost exclusively between Truro and Falmouth, daily from early June until late September.

In 1903, William Thomas took delivery of a new 113·49t.g. tug, the *Emperor*(3). She was used solely for towage in Falmouth Harbour, under the command of G. Green, ex-Master of the *Victor*. In much the same way as the *Victoria*(1) had been sold, the *Victoria*(2) was purchased in 1905 by an agent acting for the Portugese Government. At the end of the season the *Victoria*, one of the finest looking steamers to have plied the River Fal, left Falmouth for the last time. Once again a replacement was ordered from the yard of Cox & Co., and once again the resulting steamer closely resembled her predecessors. But this time a whole season elapsed before she appeared, and when she did finally enter service, the one most striking difference was to be seen in her funnel colouring. During 1906, W.J. Thomas' River Fal Steamship Company amalgamated their

interests with those of the opposing Truro registered passenger fleet of Benney & Co. Incorporated as the River Fal Steamship Co Ltd. of 1906, it was this Company that eventually took delivery of Thomas' steamer in 1907, and it was the Benney & Co. tri-colour funnel, adopted by the Company, which was worn by the new passenger steamer, the *Princess Victoria*.

BENNEY & CO.

The origin of Benney & Co.'s first passenger tug, the *Resolute*, was traced in Chapter One. In 1882 Richard Benney and his fellow shareholders in the *Resolute*, took delivery of their second passenger tug, the *New Resolute*. She was built of wood by Messrs Scoble and Davies of Malpas and measured 39·77t.g., 71·25 x 15·1 x 6·7ft. Her two cylinder compound inverted engine was supplied by Cox & Co. James Benney was appointed Master and the Mate was James' son, Albert Edward.

Richard Benney, the leading shareholder and Managing Owner of the two steamers, lived with his wife, Sarah and their son Edward in St Mary's Street, near the Cathedral in Truro. Richard's brother, James Cornelius Benney, his wife Ellen and their son Albert Edward, lived at No.15 Harbour Terrace, Falmouth. Their next door neighbours at No.14 were Philip and Caroline Thomas, with their son, William John. Capt. Daniel Benney, brother of Richard and James, also lived in Harbour Terrace and served as Master of the *New Resolute* during the 1880s. In later years the next generation of the Benney family, Ernest, James (jnr), Frederick and Richard (jnr) are each listed as crewmen aboard Benney & Co's and the River Fal Steamship Co Ltd's steamers.

By the 1890s Sarah Pollock Benney had taken over as Managing Owner of the two steamers, following the death of Richard. The official returns of the *Resolute* lists the vessel's trade as 'taking passengers to Falmouth from Truro and towing'. The *New Resolute*'s trade is similarly listed, but extends her area of operation to Fowey. She also offered excursions to the Lizard.

THE QUEEN OF THE FAL (1893)

In 1893 Sarah Benney took delivery of a third steamer, the first to bear the famous name, *Queen*

---

*After the First World War, Richard Berriman Chellew established the R B Chellew Steam Navigation Co Ltd. In 1920 illness forced Richard Chellew to give up management of the company and he was succeeded by Frank Shearman, manager of the Mount Stuart Dry Docks of Cardiff. The company's registered office was subsequently removed to Bute Town, Cardiff.

of the Fal. The steel, single screw steamer was built by Cox & Co. and registered in Truro. She measured 62·06t.g., 81·6 x 16·7 x 7·2ft. Her inverted compound engine and boiler were also built by Cox. Sarah Benney initially owned all 64 of her shares, but on 28th August 1893, eight shares each were sold to William Scoble and John Davies. Four shares each were transferred to Edward, Daniel, Ellen and Albert Edward Benney. In 1899 Sarah Benney relinquished her management of the *Queen of the Fal* when she transferred her remaining shares in all three steamers to other members of the family. Since 1897 A.E. Benney had been designated as Managing Owner of the *New Resolute*, the vessel which he also commanded for many years.

The *Resolute* was withdrawn from passenger service and in May 1902 was sold out of the Benney family's ownership. Her Truro registry finally closed after the steamer foundered in the English Channel on 4th September 1920, whilst working for the Ministry of War Transport. From April until October the *Queen of the Fal* and the *New Resolute* plied daily between Truro and Falmouth—Sundays excepted. In 1900 the return fare was one shilling, 9d single and child 6d. One intermediate call was made at Malpas, which also served as the Truro terminus at low tide, with a wagonette connection to the city. Although the timetable varied, dependent upon the tides, two morning and two afternoon runs were invariably maintained. On 20th April 1900, for example, with low tide at midday, the first steamer departed from Falmouth for Truro at 8.00AM, returning at 9.30AM. The next boat left Falmouth for Malpas only at 11.00AM, returning at noon. Another Malpas run from Falmouth at 2.30PMp.m., returning at 3.30PM, was followed by the return of the tide and a final trip to Truro at 5.00PM, returning at 6.30PM. Special evening 'moonlight' trips were offered on the Fal, departing from Falmouth for Truro or Malpas at 7.30PM, and returning by 10.00PM. 'Moonlight' trips were also made to the Black Rock, in the mouth of the Carrick Roads, proceeding to St Anthony before returning. All of the daily harbour trips and charters, to the Plum Gardens, Gatley's Quay, Mylor Creek, etc., were maintained by the second steamer. The vessels could also be hired for excursions within the Start Point—Penzance limits. Regular public coastal excursions however, seem to have worked the coast between the limits of Looe, to the east, and Porthleven, in Mounts Bay, on the western shore of the Lizard Peninsula.

THE RIVER FAL STEAMSHIP CO.LTD AND THE PRINCESS VICTORIA

In March 1906, following agreement between W.J. Thomas for the River Fal Steamship Company and A.E. Benney for Benney & Company, the *Queen of the Fal* and the *New Resolute* were sold to Gerald F. Nalder, the Falmouth solicitor engaged in the formation of the River Fal Steamship Co.Ltd. Ownership was subsequently transferred to that Company upon its incorporation. One year later the 'Benney' steamers were joined by Thomas' contribution, the replacement for the *Victoria*(2),a new 67.48t.g., steel, twin screw, passenger steamer named the *Princess Victoria*. Built by Cox & Co., the new vessel measured 81·5 x 18·8 x 6·5ft. She was powered by two Cox built inverted, compound, surface condensing engines. The *Princess Victoria* was registered at Truro, with A.E. Benney and W.J. Thomas listed as joint managing owners. Capt. George Stoddern was given command, with a crew drawn almost exclusively from the Benney family, including James Benney (jnr) as engineer. H.J.R. Corlyon of Rowe & Corlyon, Shipping & Estate Agents, was appointed as Company Secretary and Agent for the new Company. The distinctive tricolour funnel of the Benney steamers was adopted, while the hulls were initially painted white, but later reverted to the local standard of french grey hull with black gunwales. Bow decorations and lining were picked out in gold (ochre), with some deck fittings, davits, stanchions and ships boats, etc., painted white. Only the Thomas family's *Victor* differed amongst the Fal's passenger steamers in having a dark green hull.

The decision of Thomas and Benney to amalgamate their interests, might have been prompted in anticipation of the increased trade promised upon completion of the new Prince of Wales Pier at Market Strand in 1905. The original landing place at Market Strand was completed in 1873. Five years later the jetty was extended and served the majority of the Fal's passenger steamers until 1905. In July 1903 a memorial stone was laid by HRH Prince of Wales at the commencement of the new pier works. The completed Prince of Wales Pier was officially opened by the Earl of Kimberley on May 9th 1905. It measures 310ft long and 36ft wide. The deck rests upon 26 circular concrete pillars, 4ft 6ins above high water.

THE QUEEN OF THE FAL 2

In November 1911 the *Queen of the Fal* was sold to owners on the River Thames, for management by the London towage company of Watkins. Her replacement, ordered immediately from Cox & Co. inevitably bore the same name when she was delivered in July 1912. She was a single screw, steel hulled steamer, measuring 71·30t.g., 81·0 x 18·5 x 7·0ft. Her inverted, compound, direct acting engine was also built by Cox. The River Fal Steamship Co Ltd's senior Captain, George Stoddern, was transferred from the *Princess Victoria* to take command, and with him came James Benney (jnr) as engineer. Eighteen years old, Richard Benney (jnr) was signed on as able seaman. Aboard both the *Princess Victoria* and the *Queen of the Fal*, the upper deck, supported upon stanchions, provided shelter for the main passenger deck. Cover could be extended over the full length of each ship by means of fore and after deck awnings, complete with attractive scalloped edges. Only the St Mawes Steam Tug & Passenger Co.Ltd saw fit to provide more substantial deck shelters aboard the *Roseland* and the *St-Mawes*. This concession to comfort probably originated with the St Mawes ferry winter service in mind. Passenger accommodation in the saloons below was virtually standard aboard all of the Fal's steamers, and similar in practice to nearly all of the Westcountry's river steamers. The forward saloon, with plain wooden seating, dispensed alcoholic refreshments, while the after saloon usually boasted plush velvet or railway rep upholstered bench seating, a table and a small counter serving teas. There appears to have been no class demarcation aboard the steamers of the Fal, but the after saloon would usually have been reserved for ladies only. The sep-

aration of the sexes extended to the forward 'Gentlemens' saloon by common consent rather than official designation. During the 1920s and 1930s these self-imposed barriers faded away. A common feature aboard all of the Fal's steamers was a collecting box for the R.N.L.I.

In photographs it is sometimes difficult to distinguish between the *Princess Victoria* and the *Queen of the Fal*. The *Princess Victoria* sported a taller funnel, while the *Queen of the Fal* possessed more pronounced tug-like lines, notably a steeper sheer to the bows. In April 1913 A.E. Benney took command of the *Queen of the Fal*, with William Richards of Penryn deputising as the certificated Master for trips beyond Falmouth Harbour. Her trade was officially described as 'towing and carrying passengers from Falmouth to Ports within the limits of Looe and Penzance'. The eastern limit of her Class 3 certificate was extended during July and August to permit visits to Plymouth.

The *Queen of the Fal* took over most of the River Fal Steamship Co Ltd's coastal excursions, with the *Princess Victoria* almost exclusively employed on the river service between Falmouth and Truro. The *New Resolute* filled in with harbour trips within the limits of Pendennis Head and St Anthony Head.

BETWEEN THE WARS

The fleet of three steamers returned to excursion sailings in the spring of 1920. For two further decades the distinctive tricolour funnels of the River Fal Steamship Co Ltd. were to remain a familiar sight at the Prince of Wales Pier. While the St Mawes Steam Tug & Passenger Co.Ltd's steamers, the *Roseland* and the *St Mawes* were respectively associated with the Percuil River steamer services and excursions to Portscatho, so the River Fal Steamship Co Ltd's steamers, the *Princess Victoria* and *Queen of the Fal* became identified with river trips to Truro and coastal trips to the Lizard, Mevagissey and Fowey. Following the sale of the *Victor* after the death of William Thomas in 1934, the *Queen of the Fal* remained as the sole visitor to the old Lizard landing places at Coverack and Church Cove. The *New Resolute* was sold out of the fleet in 1927, a victim perhaps of the economies forced upon the steamer operators, resulting from the steep rise in coal prices following the miners and General Strike in 1926. Albert Benney bought the steamer privately,

for use as a tug in connection with his family's remaining shipping interests. She was subsequently owned by Harvey's, the timber merchants of Truro, and later by Messrs Roberts and Burt, bargeowners of Tresillian. The *New Resolute* was scrapped on the mud flats at Tresillian by the Roberts brothers, in 1946.

At the outbreak of the Second World War in September 1939, all excursions ceased and the River Fal Steamship Co.Ltd. closed down their daily operations. On 30th January 1942 the *Princess Victoria* was acquired by the Ministry of War Transport. Likewise the *Queen of the Fal* was purchased in March of the same year. Both steamers left the Fal, never to return. It would appear that the steamers served at Greenock, tendering to ships in the Clyde, but further details concerning their eventual fate have proved difficult to trace. The River Fal Steamship Co.Ltd was subsequently wound up, creating a post war 'vacuum' that was to be contested by a succession of motor launch fleets, and eventually filled by the 'Enterprise' fleet which maintains the Truro service today.

The *Victor* steams out of Falmouth Harbour towards the coast. Just visible in the background, off Trefusis, is the *Princess Victoria*, making her way out to the Carrick Roads.

Photo: E A Bragg; A K collection

The *Victor*, on the left, and the *Dragon* towing a listing ship into Falmouth Docks. While the *Victor* doubled as a passenger steamer, the *Dragon* sought additional employment as a trawler. Part of her number FH216 can be seen on her funnel.
Photo: E A Bragg; Royal Institution of Cornwall

Frederick Martin was the engineer aboard the *Victor* for 36 years. He is pictured here at Gyllingvase Beach with his grandson.
Photo courtesy Mr H Leslie Martin

Capt. Stoddern in the wheelhouse of the *Princess Victoria*.
Roy Stribley collection

Photographs of Messrs Chard and Thomas'
passenger tug, the *Victoria* of 1900, are very
rare, plying in the district as she did for just
six months. She is pictured here in
Falmouth Harbour, with the villas of
Trefusis Road, Flushing, in the background.
Roy Stribley collection

The second *Victoria* entered service in June 1901. She is easily distinguished from her predecessor by the provision of an upper deck. Photographed at Malpas, her passengers are landing by small boats.

Royal Institution of Cornwall

TRURO RIVER

The *Queen of the Fal* off Trennick Row on the Truro River, before 1906. The warehouses at Truro can be seen in the background. The *Queen of the Fal* had a poop deck, providing extra headroom for the after saloon. Cox & Co employed a similar feature aboard the *Princess May*, which they built for the St Mawes Steam Tug & Passenger Co Ltd.

Royal Institution of Cornwall

The River Fal Steamship Company's *Victoria* and Benney & Company's *Queen of the Fal*, moored alongside Town Quay, Truro, c1901-04.

Royal Institution of Cornwall

The *Queen of the Fal* and the *Roseland* at Market Strand, prior to 1903. At least twelve topsail schooners are moored off Flushing, in the background.

Royal Institution of Cornwall

TRURO WESLEYAN OUTING 1908. AT TRURO QUAY. Nº 3

The *New Resolute* and the *Queen of the Fal* embarking a Truro Wesleyan outing at Worth's Quay in 1908. Schooners, ketches and barges once lined Trafalgar Wharf—now known as Phoenix Wharf—in the background.

Royal Institution of Cornwall

Aboard the *New Resolute* at Truro. Harveys timber warehouses can be seen behind. The skipper is thought to be Albert Edward Benney.

Roy Stribley collection

Upon the incorporation of the River Fal Steamship Co Ltd in 1906, the ex-Benney steamers were repainted with white hulls. The *New Resolute* is pictured at Malpas in 1906 or 1907.
Photo: E A Bragg; A K collection

Photographed at Prince of Wales Pier in 1906/7 the *Queen of the Fal* sports more than just a new hull colour, having been substantially rebuilt with the addition of an upper deck.

The old stone courses of Market Strand Quay are clearly discernable below the newer granite courses which form the approach to the new pier. Stonework incorporated into the walls of the basin at the pier entrance dates from the days when this part of Falmouth's waterfront was the main quay of Smithwick Harbour.
Photo: E A Bragg; A K collection

The new *Princess Victoria* of 1907 leaving Truro during her first or second year of operation.

Photo: E A Bragg; A K collection

Within two years the River Fal Steamship Co Ltd's fleet of three steamers reverted to the old Benney & Co hull colours of French grey hull and black gunwhales. The *Princess Victoria* is pictured in the Carrick Roads, with Falmouth Bay in the distance ahead.

Photo E A Bragg; A K collection

The crew of the *Princess Victoria* from the right to left: Capt George Stoddern, Frederick Benney and James Benney (behind). The two remaining crewmen are unidentified, but seated in front is believed to be Ernest Benney.

Roy Stribley collection

Used solely as a tug on the Truro River following her sale out of the River Fal Steamship Co Ltd's fleet in 1927, the *New Resolute* is pictured attending a timber ship at Woodbury buoy, presumably whilst in the ownership of Harvey's, the timber merchants, at Truro.

Photo: Osborne's of Falmouth

The second *Queen of the Fal* entered service in 1912. Her similarity to the *Princess Victoria* is evident from this photograph, taken from the Prince of Wales Pier. However, below the waterline the two steamers differed totally. The design of the *Queen of the Fal* incorporated a deep draught and a large single propeller. While this rendered her more efficient as a tug, it also severely restricted her visits to the shallow Truro River. In common with the two *Victoria*'s, the *Princess Victoria* was driven with twin screws. This helped to counter the loss of draught necessary for working the Truro River. These design differences are the main contributory factor for the *Princess Victoria* maintaining the Truro River services and the *Queen of the Fal* working the coastal excursions.

Royal Institution of Cornwall

Photographed from Town Quay, the *Princess Victoria* approaches Worth's Quay, c1912; the tall warehouse behind was built in 1911.

In many photographs reproduced in this book, the steamers tow a small boat with a man aboard. Unfortunately no simple answer has been forthcoming to explain this practice. The answer might lay in a combination of reasons. Where landings were to be made by boat, it might well have been simpler for the oarsman to travel in this fashion. There was also a well tried practice amongst vessels plying in shallow water, of towing a man in a boat so that a rope could always be put ashore quickly, or a kedge anchor run out, for the purpose of winching the vessel off the mud in the event of a grounding. In some instances the boatman might simply have accepted a tow.

Royal Institution of Cornwall

CHAPTER FOUR

COASTAL EXCURSIONS

To stand today upon the steeply sloping slipway of Church Cove, Landewednack, beside its disused lifeboat station and old pilchard cellars, it is difficult to appreciate any direct link with the story of Cornwall's passenger craft. But for many years the Fal steamers called to land their passengers in this tiny cove below Lizard Town. From here the intrepid trippers climbed the steep track, pausing perhaps to take tea at the picturesque thatched cottages, before continuing on foot or by wagonette to view the breathtaking scenery of Kynance Cove, or to visit the Lizard Lighthouse and Southernmost Point. Later, as departure time approached, the steamer's whistle was blown, sending thousands of seagulls wheeling and crying into the air, an adequate warning to excursionists within a wide radius. Returning through Lizard Town, souvenirs were purchased from one of the serpentine stone workshops that are still unique to the southern tip of the Lizard Peninsula. It is perhaps not entirely coincidental that such workshops were established in Lizard Town, Southernmost Point and Church Cove, during the late 19th century, when the *Emperor* and the *New Resolute* first began regular calls. Back at the cove the visitors were taken off, as they had been landed, by boats, a precarious practice that the modern observer might find hard to imagine amidst such uncompromising surroundings. Not for excursionists along the Cornish coast were to be found the piers, pavilions, promenades and funfairs offered elsewhere in the country. No such frivolous attrac-

tions were deemed necessary to 'add' to the natural beauty. No seasonal paddle steamers pierced this rugged coastline, to visit its tiny coves and jetties. But the local passenger tugs that had evolved on the Fal proved eminently suitable for the purpose, embodying as they did the necessary sea going qualities called for in the towage trade. For over sixty years the Fal steamers offered excursions along this coastline, working in perfect harmony with their surroundings and providing the most exciting method of visiting otherwise isolated villages along the south Cornwall coast. These excursions were enjoyed by locals and visitors alike, many travelling by rail from as far afield as St Austell and Penzance for the day. The selection could be bewildering, intending trippers for the week commencing 2nd June 1913, could choose between the *Alexandra*'s visits to the Lizard, Porthoustock, Coverack and Helford, departing either from St Mawes or Falmouth; the *New Resolute* and the *Queen of the Fal*'s visits to Looe, Fowey, Mevagissey, Porthleven, Lizard (Church Cove), Porthoustock, Helford and Gweek; or the *Victor* which was calling at Church Cove and other Lizard landing places, completing the week with a long trip to Plymouth, for the Regatta.

Sadly, for the past fifty years such regular coastal excursions have no longer been available.

THE HELFORD RIVER

In addition then to the development of local passenger steamer services upon the complex system of waterways within the Pendennis Point−St Anthony

Point limits, there evolved purely excursion trade along virtually the entire south Cornwall coast. To the west the steamers plied across Falmouth Bay to visit the Helford River, the Lizard Peninsula and around Lizard Point into Mounts Bay. In the east calls were made to villages in Gerrans, Veryan and St Austell Bays, and further afield to Fowey, Looe and Plymouth.

Passenger craft with a Class 4 certificate could (and still can, subject to weather and other conditions) ply to the Helford River. The river is an estuary fed by a multitude of small streams. There is hardly one reach or inlet of the Helford that could be described as anything less than beautiful. From the mouth of the estuary to the heads of each individual creek, the waterborne visitor is presented with some of the most picturesque and tranquil scenery in Cornwall.

In common with the neighbouring Fal, the Helford River once served as a tidal highway. Trading vessels called at the various quays scattered along its shore-line, serving local villages, estates and farms. Ketches and barges trading to the Glendurgan Estate

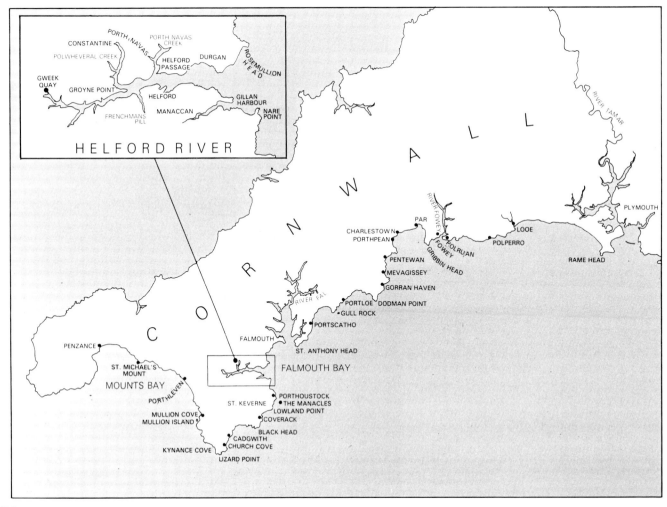

landed on the small beach at Durgan. This small community hosted the local regatta, to which the *Emperor* brought spectators from Falmouth. Passengers were regularly landed at the pretty Port Navas Quay, in Port Navas Creek, well known for its Duchy of Cornwall Oyster Farm. The steamers also plied the adjacent Polwheveral, or Calamansack, Creek, with the village of Constantine at its head. There was no steamer landing in the creek, but until 1906 a local trading ketch, the *Rob Roy*, served the little quay at Merthen. She was owned by John Tyack of Merthen Manor, whose family had for centuries held the rights to the Helford Ferry, which crossed the estuary between the Ferryboat Inn at Helford Passage (or just 'Passage') to Helford on the Meneage shore. Regular excursions calls were made at Helford, the steamer anchored offshore while the passengers were landed by the ferry boat and/or the ship's boat. This was usually the highest point of navigation for both the *Emperor* and the *Victor*. Steamers sometimes landed trippers at Helford for the day. The nearby church at Manaccan, a great favourite with such visitors, was renowned for the fig tree growing out of the tower wall. Today the adjacent Frenchman's Creek (or Frenchman's Pill), made famous by the novelist Daphne du Maurier, arouses more interest from waterborne visitors. At Groyne Point, the estuary divides. Polwheveral Creek reaches away due north, while the main channel continues to the inland village of Gweek, at the head of navigation, over three miles further upstream from Helford. Gweek Quay remained relatively busy as an agricultural distribution point well into the 20th century. Local river barges, coastal ketches and schooners such as the *Rylands*, *Emma & Esher* and *Haldon*, numbered amongst the vessels still calling during the 1920s. Around this time one or two motor launches appeared on the estuary. They were licensed to carry twelve passengers and additionally available for a tow to Gweek. Passenger steamers calling at Gweek sometimes anchored offshore, but near spring tides landings alongside the quay itself were specially noted in advertisements.

The *New Resolute*, both *Queens of the Fal* and the St Mawes company's *Alexandra*, once plied to Gweek. More recently, during the 1960s, Joseph and Sidney Timmins' 51ft motor vessel, the *Queen of Helford*, has specialised in this trade, as the largest passenger vessel plying to Gweek Quay. During the 1980s the MV *St Gerrans*, in the ownership of the Cornish Ferry (Red Funnel) Co.Ltd has remained alone in providing excursions to the Helford River, a river she first plied over 60 years ago for the St-Mawes Steam Tug & Passenger Co.Ltd.

THE LIZARD

It was appropriate that each of the Fal's passenger steamers carried a collecting box for the R.N.L.I., as all of their landing places on the Lizard Peninsula— Porthoustock, Coverack, Church Cove, Polpeor Cove, Mullion Cove and Porthleven—have either been lifeboat stations or housed lifeboats.* Polpeor Cove offered a secondary landing for the passenger steamers, immediately below Southernmost Point, and was used when weather conditions rendered Church Cove unsuitable. In common with the landing at Church Cove, boats were also used to land passengers at Porthoustock on the Lizard Peninsula's eastern shore. Here, too, trippers faced a steep climb if they wished to visit the nearby village of St Keverne. The foreshore at Porthoustock could (and still can) present a bleak impression, dominated as it was by the quarries and loading shute jetties of the West of England Road Metal Co.Ltd. These were the jetties at which barges plying to Tresillian Quay loaded. The contrast between the sylvan setting of the Tresillian River and this desolate cove near the deadly Manacle Rocks, could not be more complete. Details gleaned from steamer advertisements in the *Falmouth Packet* reveal the localised nature of some Porthoustock excursions. On Thursday July 12th, 1900, the *New Resolute* made a special visit for the 'opening of the new organ' at the Wesleyan Chapel in St Keverne. The landing al-

---

* The first lifeboat station on the Lizard was established in Polpeor Cove in 1859. In 1867 stations were established at Mullion Cove and Cadgwith. In Church Cove was housed a second boat for the Lizard (Polpeor) crew, but only two service launches were ever made from this boathouse. In 1961 the Lizard and Cadgwith stations amalgamated to work from a new station in Kilcobben Cove. This station alone serves the Lizard coast today.

lowed time for passengers to enjoy the public luncheon, organ recital, prayer meeting and tea. On June 26th, 1913 (and annually), the *Queen of the Fal* called specially for the St Keverne Agricultural Show. Since the turn of the century a visit to the *Mohegan* Memorial in St Keverne, provided a poignant reminder of the unforgiving coast along which the Fal steamers plied.

Until the turn of the century, beach landings were undertaken at Kynance Cove by the *Emperor*, which similarly landed passengers onto Mullion Island. Elsewhere along the Lizard coast, trippers enjoyed comparatively comfortable landings directly onto the stone jetties at Coverack, Mullion Cove and Porthleven.

The *Queen of the Fal*(2) and the *Alexandra* offered at least one Penzance trip each summer. During 1905-6 a more substantial service between the two ports was maintained by the West Cornwall Steamship Company's Isles of Scilly steamer, the RMS *Deerhound*. She was a steel twin screw vessel measuring 482t.g., 189·0 x 26·1 x 9·5ft. The *Deerhound* is undoubtedly the largest passenger steamer to have come alongside at the Prince of Wales Pier. Her departures from Falmouth were in fact the return leg of an all day Penzance Falmouth trip. Her Falmouth passengers returned by rail at an inclusive price of 3s.6d. Other interlopers included the Saltash, Three Towns & District Steamboat Co.Ltd's paddle steamer, the *Princess Royal*. She arrived light on Falmouth Regatta days, to provide public or charter trips to view the events. Ocean liner tenders from Plymouth offered an extensive excursion programme, cruising along the South Cornwall coast and calling in at Falmouth regularly. Their South Devon passengers went ashore for two hours and Channel excursions were offered in the interim, departing from the Western Breakwater of Falmouth Docks. The G.W.R. tenders, *Sir Richard Grenville* (1891) and the *Antelope*, and the London & South Western Railway Company's *Victoria*, from Ocean Quay, Stonehouse, were included amongst these visitors.

The *Victor* until 1933, and then the *Queen of the Fal* alone until 1939, were the last steamers to maintain Church Cove calls. In 1927 the St Mawes Steam Tug & Passenger Co.Ltd's new motor vessel, the *St Gerrans*, was restricted to plying within the Black Head limit. Sixty years later she alone has offered occasional excursions to the Lizard Peninsula, landing at Coverack.

THE SOUTH EAST COAST OF CORNWALL

Along the coast to the east of the Carrick Roads, the Fal steamers maintained regular excursions as far as Looe and occasionally to Plymouth. Both the *Victor* and, for a short period, William Rowe's *Penguin*, were once to be found attending virtually every regatta along Cornwall's south east coast.

In Gerrans Bay, Portscatho remained the exclusive domain of the St Mawes company. Steamers from St Mawes and Falmouth cruised to Gull Rock, off Nare Head and then steamed across Gerrans Bay to land passengers by boat at Portscatho for about two hours. Excepting the *Roseland*, all of the St Mawes company's steamers have called at Portscatho. Occasional visits were made to the pretty fishing village of Portloe, in Veryan Bay.

Mevagissey was a popular and regular destination for trippers out of Falmouth and Plymouth alike. Many summer Saturday afternoons and evenings found excursion steamers from both ports moored alongside the outer breakwater. Calls were also made at Porthpean and Charlestown, usually to coincide with special events in nearby St Austell. Once the steamer had completed her St Austell Bay landings she headed for her next port of call at Fowey, where passengers were landed at the Town Quay. Trippers were usually allowed two hours ashore, and in the interim the Falmouth steamer sometimes offered an additional excursion to view Polperro and Looe. On 3rd June 1931, while she was engaged upon a Mevagissey-Fowey-Looe run, the *Queen of the Fal*, with thirty passengers aboard, encountered fog. Having safely navigated Dodman Point, she proceeded to Mevagissey, but was too close to the shore to clear the next promontory, Cadythew Rock. She went aground on the rock strewn shore of Vault Beach, near Gorran Haven, but disaster was narrowly averted when she miraculously came to rest between rocks, on the sandy beach. Ironically she lay just yards from a coastguard lookout and the coastguard station at Gorran Haven. The Fowey lifeboat, the *C.D.E.C.* was called out, attached a towline and waited off shore in a calm sea for the tide to return. Two hours later the *Queen of the Fal* was afloat again and able to return to Falmouth undamaged and under her own steam.

Trips to Plymouth were undertaken on special occasions. The *Emperor* went for the 'Swimming Matches' on Wednesday August 13th 1890, landing at the Promenade Pier. the trip started at 7.30AM and arrived back at 9.00PM On Monday July 7th 1900, the *Victor* departed for Plymouth from Market Strand Quay at 6.30AM, on a special charter for the Falmouth Foundry Men's outing; the fare was two shillings. The *Victor* also attended some Plymouth Regattas, offering five hours ashore to enjoy the fun fairs and other events on Plymouth Hoe. Rail return tickets were available aboard the ocean liner tenders, *en route* to Mevagissey, Fowey, Looe and Plymouth, on the return leg of their day excursion to Falmouth.

Since the Second World War, long distance coastal excursions have been few and far between. In 1946, Coast Lines Ltd purchased the 306t.g. twin screw excursion steamer, the *Robina*. She was reportedly intended for use as a coastal excursion ship at Falmouth. However, Coast Lines decided instead to charter her to their subsidiary David MacBrayne on the west coast of Scotland. For the 1949/50/51 seasons a converted, ex-naval, Fairmile 'B' launch, named the *Pendennis*, plied the immediate Cornish coast. The 119t.g., twin screw, wooden vessel was on charter to the Falmouth Boat Building Company from the Blackpool Steam Navigation Co (1947) Ltd. In November 1963 another converted Fairmile 'B' launch, the *Kiloran II*, was acquired from the Devon Cruising Company of Torquay by the Cornish Sea Cruising Company. For a few seasons she offered a five hour cruise along some sixty miles of the Cornish coast and also visited the Helford. She was based at St Mawes. The two above named boats were built at Teddington and Maldon respectively. Its worth noting, however, that the Falmouth Boat Construction Company built ten Fairmile 'B's for the Admiralty during the Second World War.

In 1984 the rare opportunity of a day excursion from Plymouth to the Lizard was offered aboard the *Waverley*, the world's last, sea-going, paddle steamer. She cruised past all of the Fal steamers' coastal haunts, Looe, Polperro, Fowey, St Austell Bay, Veryan Bay and Gerrans Bay. The paddler was greeted by hundreds of additional passengers embarking at Falmouth for the trip to the Lizard Point. The *Waverley* continued across Falmouth Bay and passed the Helford River, Porthoustock and Coverack. As she turned in a very choppy sea off the Lizard Point, Church Cove could just be sighted below Lizard Town. This, I suspect is now the nearest that excursionists will ever get to the Fal steamer's old landing place on the southernmost tip of the British mainland.

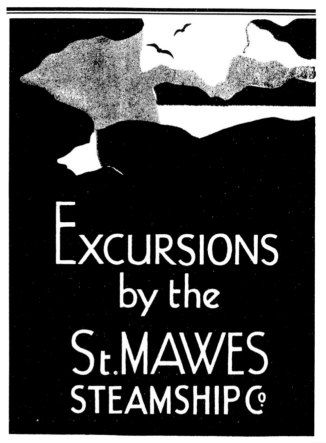

EXCURSIONS by the St.MAWES STEAMSHIP Co

The *Queen of the Fal* anchored off Church Cove during the early 1930s. Returning passengers are being rowed out to the steamer.
Photo: Hawke of Helston; A K collection

At low tide passengers were landed onto Battleship Rock and left to pick their way ashore over the slippery rocks. The *Victor* is pictured landing her passengers in this fashion, c1930. The headland on the horizon is the Black Head.
Photo: Hawke of Helston; A K collection

Looking towards the serpentine cave of
Dolor Hugo and Cadgwith, from Church
Cove. The *Queen of the Fal* lies at anchor,
awaiting the return of her passengers.
Photo: J Valentine; A K collection

The first *Queen of the Fal* steaming past
Helford Passage, c1910.
Photo: E A Bragg; A K collection

The Helford Estuary, c1890. On the eastern (left) shore, at the mouth of the estuary is Toll Point. The bay on the left is Polgwidden Cove, the land is part of the Glendurgan Estate. Helford Passage lies out of shot to the left. The passenger tug *Emperor* is anchored off Helford, the village lies off to the right. The shallow inlet behind is Treath, the private jetty reached deep water at all stages of the tide, but was not used by the steamers.

Photo: J Valentine; courtesy Royal Institution of Cornwall

Photographs of steamers at Gweek are rare; here the *Queen of the Fal* is pictured alongside Gweek Quay, on a spring tide during the 1930s. The small open boat moored astern of the steamer is possibly one of the motor launches, or 'motor quay punts' as one schooner skipper described them, that were licenced to carry twelve passengers and also piloted and towed vessels up to Gweek.

In 1796 there was a scheme for a canal to link the Helford and the Hayle Rivers. A report was drawn up by the famous engineer Robert Fulton. Plans of the proposed route are deposited in the County Records Office at Truro. Had the canal been built, one wonders whether Helston, St Erth, Hayle and St Ives might not have featured amongst the excursion destinations on offer from Falmouth!

A K collection

An unidentified motor launch makes her way up Port Navas Creek in the early 1950s.
A K collection

The *Victor* anchored off Porthoustock. The quarry and loading shute jetties of the West of England Road Metal Co Ltd dominate the shoreline. In the foreground is the lifeboat station. The road up to St Keverne leads off to the right.

Photo: E A Bragg; A K collection

The *Queen of the Fal* (1) passes the Manacle Rocks off Porthoustock.
Photo: *E A Bragg; A K collection*

The *Queen of the Fal* (2) at Coverack Pier in the 1930s.
A K collection

The Isles of Scilly steamer RMS *Deerhound* at the Prince of Wales Pier in 1906. She awaits her passengers for the return leg of her excursion from Penzance. The *Victor* is anchored on the opposite side of the pier, while the *Queen of the Fal* can be seen departing.

Photo: E A Bragg; A K collection

The paddle steamer *Princess Royal* was owned by the Saltash Three Towns & District Steamboat Co Ltd on the River Tamar. From the Plymouth district this paddler offered excursions along the South Devon coast to Salcombe and to Mevagissey in Cornwall. Visits to Falmouth were made light on regatta days, for the purpose of engaging charters to view the days events. Also moored at Market Strand Quay is the Flushing Ferry steamer *Greyhound* and one of the St Mawes steamers.

Photo: J Valentine; A K collection

Landing passengers at Portscatho, from the steamer *St Mawes*. In the distance is Nare Head and Gull Rock.

Roy Stribley collection

EXCURSION STEAMERS, MEVAGISSEY

The St Mawes Steam Tug & Passenger
Co Ltd's excursion steamer *Alexandra*,
moored at Mevagissey's outer breakwater
in 1909. Astern lies the G W R's ocean liner
tender, the *Sir Richard Grenville*, on an
excursion from Plymouth.
Photo: S Dalby Smith of St Blazey;
A K collection

Passengers aboard the *Queen of the Fal* in 1923.

Royal Institution of Cornwall

The converted ex-Naval Fairmile 'B' launch *Kiloran II* off Prince of Wales Pier. During the 1960s this vessel offered a five hour cruise viewing the Cornish coast. Built by J Sadd of Maldon in 1941, the launch was converted to a private yacht, named the *Lepanto*, in 1951. In 1956 she was offering cruises from Conway, re-named the *Cambrian Prince*. One year later she was sold to the Devon Cruising Company of Torquay to replace their coastal cruising vessel, the *Kiloran*. She was acquired by the Cornish Sea Cruising Company of St Mawes in 1963.

Photo: John Clarkson

The *Tudor Prince* of the Cornish Ferry (Red Funnel) Co Ltd, is pictured in Fowey Harbour in 1984. She was chartered by Jaguar to view the annual power boat race between Falmouth and Fowey. Sadly, regular public coastal excursions are no longer available from Falmouth. Nigel Godfrey, skipper of the *Tudor Prince*, explained that the strict safety conditions demanded by the Board of Trade coupled with a lack of public interest, rendered such trips unprofitable.

The Fowey tug, *Gribbin Head* which lies ahead has recently been sold. In the background is the village of Polruan.

Photo: A K

CHAPTER FIVE

POST WAR MOTOR VESSELS

The declaration of war in September 1939 effectively ended the history of steam engined passenger vessels on the Fal. The steamers, *Queen of the Fal*, *Princess Victoria*, and the *St Mawes*, were each requisitioned for war service in 1942, never to return to Cornish waters. By the end of the war the *Roseland* too had been withdrawn. This abrupt end to the steam era contrasts sharply with the previously slow acceptance of internal combustion engines for passenger boats on the Fal. It is the purpose of this final chapter to continue the story of the St Mawes and Flushing ferry services, and to briefly review the main post war motor vessel operators who sought to inherit the Fal's passenger trade from the River Fal Steamship Co.Ltd.

THE ST MAWES FERRY

Within four years of the end of the war, the St-Mawes Steam Tug & Passenger Co.Ltd returned their depleted fleet to full strength with the acquisition of two new motor vessels. In 1948 the *St Gerrans* and the *New Roseland* were joined by the 75t.g. steel motor vessel *St Mawes Castle*. She was built by Philip of Dartmouth and measured 70 x 18·2 x 6ft. Her diesel engines were supplied by Blackstone & Co Ltd. of London. The second new boat, purchased in 1950, was a 52ft long motor vessel named the *New Princess Maud*. For eighteen years this fleet remained unchanged and throughout the 1950s and 1960s continued to offer passenger services on the Fal, Percuil and Helford rivers.

In 1967 control of the St Mawes Steam Tug & Passenger Co.Ltd passed to two new directors, Norman and Thomas Smith. Thomas Treloar of Arwenack

Manor (Assistant Secretary of the old St Mawes Steam Tug & Passenger Co.) was designated as Managing Owner of the company's vessels at this time and in the spring of 1968 he put the entire fleet up for auction at Mylor Yacht Harbour. The motor vessels *St Gerrans* and *St Mawes Castle* were eventually sold to Thames Pleasure Craft Ltd. The *New Roseland* remained on the Fal for two further years before she, too, was sold for service on the Thames with Coakley's Launches. Only the little launch the *New Princess Maud* survived to continue on the St Mawes ferry.

After a century providing passenger steamer services in the Falmouth district, the St Mawes Steam Tug & Passenger Co.Ltd finally withdrew from operation and was subsequently wound up. The Smith brothers incorporated a new company, the St-Mawes Ferry Co.Ltd, in 1970. Control of this company passed successively to Mr Wm.S. Miller in 1971, and to Leslie W. Ancliffe, a retired army officer of Appledore, in 1975. The St Mawes Ferry Co Ltd. offered no excursions, maintaining only the St-Mawes ferry service from the Prince of Wales Pier. Calls to Percuil and St Anthony had been withdrawn for a number of years. The ferry fleet comprised of three vessels; the ex-St Mawes Steam Tug & Passenger Co Ltd's *New Princess Maud*, and two additional wooden motor vessels, the *Princess Maria* and an open launch the *Princess Marina*. In 1976 the St Mawes Ferry Co Ltd. acquired the ex-Flushing Ferry boat, *Nankersey*. Within twelve months the Company purchased two ex-Dartmouth Harbour ferry boats from British Rail at a cost of £14,000.

These two sister vessels, the *Adrian Gilbert* and the *Humphrey Gilbert*, each measured 35t.g., 57·9 x 13·5 x 4·9ft. They were intended to replace the Company's four boats (collectively valued at £15,000), but were reportedly considered unsuitable for the St Mawes crossing. Whether by prior agreement or just good fortune, the two boats were almost immediately repurchased for exactly the same price by British Rail, who had decided to try them instead on their own Gravesend-Tilbury Ferry. There is some doubt as to whether these two motor vessels ever actually came to the Fal!

The ferry company's four boats were sold off in 1978 to Mr T.E. Mattocks of St Just. The St Mawes Ferry Co Ltd. continued as a non-trading registered Company until it was dissolved in 1986. The St Mawes ferry is not a statutory route like that between Flushing and Falmouth. Successive operators therefore could never claim exclusive rights. Each time the St Mawes ferry boat fleet has changed hands their trade or 'goodwill' has followed. When the St-Mawes Steam Tug & Passenger Co Ltd. sold its fleet in 1968, the Pill family of Falmouth seized the opportunity to introduce their own motor vessel, the *May Queen*, onto the route. The resulting, sometimes heated, competition between successive owners of the St Mawes fleet and the 'interloper' was resolved when the Pill family agreed to run between St-Mawes and Town Quay in Falmouth, surrendering the Prince of Wales Pier to the St Mawes boats. This arrangement continues today.

In 1980 the St Mawes fleet changed hands again and Mr Peter Sparkes operated the fleet, trading as the St Mawes Ferry Company. The three ferry boats in regular use are: the *Nankersey* (89 passengers); the *New Princess Maud* (113 passengers); and the *Princess Maria* (100 passengers). A thirty minute service is provided throughout the summer season. A reduced frequency is maintained during the winter. In 1987 the fleet changed hands once again!

THE FLUSHING FERRY

In January 1940 Robert Kessel sold the *Miranda II* to John Messer Bennets of Devoran, a Truro solicitor who also held a directorship in the King Harry Steam Ferry Ltd. Within two months the Flushing Ferry Ltd

was incorporated with the objects '. . . . . to acquire and take over as a going concern the motor ferry at present maintained by John Messer Bennets [and] to acquire the lease of the ferry and/or ferry rights between Old Quay at Flushing and the Prince of Wales Pier, Falmouth.' The directors of the new company were: J.M. Bennets; Col.The Hon.Henry Walter Hepburn Stuart Forbes Trefusis (owner of the Ferry rights); and Harry Sylvanus Austin Johns, an oyster fishing proprietor, of Fore Street, Flushing. In addition to being the largest shareholder, Harry Johns was also appointed as manager of the new company. In July 1951 the Flushing Ferry Ltd's share capital was increased to help finance the building of a new boat. Suitably named the *Nankersey* (the name of the original community, supplanted by Flushing), the new wooden motor vessel was built by Falmouth Boat Construction. She measured 23t.g., 45 x 13·8 x 5·7ft. The Berguis company of Glasgow supplied her Kelvin diesel engines. During the early 1960s, Mr A.C. Vissick of the Basset Works, Devoran, was listed both as Managing Owner of the *Nankersey* and Public Officer of the Flushing Ferry Ltd.

In common with the St Mawes ferry, the Flushing service in recent years has endured a succession of owners. In 1970, Anthony Lloyd, Jean Parker of Flushing, and Robert Sanders of Helston, gained control of the Flushing Ferry Ltd. The *Nankersey* was sold locally and currently plies for the St Mawes Ferry Company. By the late 1970s Jean Parker and Colin Parker (boatman) controlled the company. In March 1981 all of the shares were sold in equal quantities to retired doctor, Dr F.E. Clynick and four members of his family.

Meanwhile, amidst all of these interminable changes of ownership, the *Miranda II* and three self-employed boatmen continued the real work of maintaining the Flushing Ferry. The Flushing Ferry Ltd ceased trading in 1984/5. F.M. Clynick of Falmouth is currently credited with ownership of the Ferry. A new boat was ordered in 1985, from A.J. Murray, Yacht & Boat Builder of Falmouth. The 28ft glass fibre motor vessel perpetuates the name *Miranda*. She carries 38 passengers and seems well suited to the work for which she was built. The *Miranda II* was sold to George Pill of Falmouth and almost immediately resold by him to Torquay owners.

RIVER EXCURSION VESSELS

With the absence of the River Fal Steamship Co Ltd's steamers during the first post war season in 1946, Rodney 'Pete' Newman of Tolverne Cottage ran a 30 seat passenger launch, the *Freelance* between Truro and Falmouth. The Newmans had moved to Tolverne from Mylor in 1934. Rodney Newman—an engineer, once employed at Vissick's Basset Foundry in Devoran—had been running a 12 seater launch, the *Mystery*, since 1937, mainly tendering to laid up shipping in the Fal.

In 1947 Victory Pleasures Ltd was incorporated to operate river services and excursions on the Fal, with three launches, *Lily of Laguna*, *Gondolier* and *Water Spry*. In the late 1940s Victory Pleasures Ltd. acquired the more substantial 40t.g., twin screw, motor vessel *Worcester Castle*. Built by M.W. Blackmore in 1926, this boat had originally worked out of Aberystwyth, but was owned by the Ministry of War Transport during the Second World War. Bookings for Victory Pleasures Ltd's river and harbour cruises could be made at Western National Coach Booking Offices. The Company provided a daily summertime service between Truro and Falmouth and also offered speedboat trips 'for service and pleasure'. In 1950 Victory Pleasures Ltd went bankrupt and the Company was dissolved. The *Lily of Laguna* was sold to the St Mary's Boatmen's Association on the Isles of Scilly, where she continues in passenger service today. The *Water Spry* was sold to George Pill of Falmouth. The *Gondolier* was acquired by the local Green Boats fleet. Finally, the *Worcester Castle* was sold to Dartmouth owners for conversion to a houseboat.

The Newmans bought an ex-Admiralty launch which Rodney Newman's son, George—who had served as a shipwright at Falmouth Boat Construction—converted to passenger service. The launch was named *Skylark*. They bought a second launch from the Channel Islands, and renamed her *Skylark II*. George Newman skippered this vessel while Rodney remained with the first *Skylark*.

Harry Johns, manager of the Flushing Ferry, meanwhile ran the launches *Moyana* and *Enterprise* on the Falmouth-Truro run. Later in 1950 he added the *Kingsley*, a passenger launch measuring 43·2 x 10·3 x 4·3ft, which had been built by T. Bulley & Son of Teignmouth in 1926. She was soon sold to the St-Mary's Boatmen's Association, as was another of Johns' later launches, the *Coronation Belle*, which survives on the Isles of Scilly as the *Black Swan*. In 1951 Johns took delivery of a brand new motor vessel. Built by Frazer & Son of Mevagissey, the boat measured 25·t.g., 50·6 x 14·9 x 6·1ft. Mr Johns resurrected the famous name *Queen of the Fal* for his new pleasure boat. In the early 1950s Harry Johns bought the 34t.g. *Sheppy Queen* of Sheerness and in 1954 acquired another new wooden, motor boat, the 60ft *Enterprise II*, built for him by M.W. Blackmore & Sons of Bideford.

The Newmans substantially increased the capacity of their little 'Skylark' fleet, when they purchased the *Worcester Castle* back from her owners on the River Dart. Only her hull survived, the engines and superstructure having been dismantled. The hull was towed down to Tolverne by a fishing boat. She was equipped with Dorman engines, rebuilt by George Newman to carry 250 passengers and fitted with a licenced bar. The passenger vessel was entered onto the Truro Register in 1954 as the *Skylark of Tolverne*. Rodney Newman died in 1960 and in July 1961 his son, George, drowned in a tragic accident at Tolverne. At only sixteen years of age, Peter Newman was too young to take over his father's and brother's business. Ownership of the boats passed to Mrs Mabel Newman, who sold them. The *Skylark* and the *Freelance* were sold privately. *Skylark II* went to the Green Boats passenger fleet. In 1962 the *Skylark of Tolverne* was sold to Colin Bewley of Paignton. After just two seasons in Torbay, during which time she had been renamed the *Beach Belle*, the motor vessel moved to West Wales, working from Tenby as the *Tenby Queen*. Although out of service for a number of years, her Truro registry was finally closed in 1983, when she was listed as being 'beyond repair'. Until 1982 the name of Newman was sadly missing amongst the passenger boat operators on the Fal. But in that year Peter Newman bought a 37ft ex-Admiralty motor launch, the *Heather*, from Messrs Hambly and Sweet of Falmouth. The launch had previously been owned by T.R. Gunn of Cowlands Creek, immediately opposite Tolverne Cottage. Maintained in an immaculate condition and skippered by Peter Newman, the *Heather* today provides return trips from Town Quay, Falmouth to land for lunch or afternoon tea at Tolverne (or Smugglers) Cottage. The cottage restaurant is well worth a visit for the virtual museum of memorabilia collected by the Newmans over the years from the multitude of ships that have been laid up in the King Harry and Tolverne Reaches. Peter Newman also runs the 12 seater launch *Polgerran*.

'Green Boats' was the trading name of the green painted launches of the River Fal & Western Cruises Ltd. This London-based company, incorporated in 1954, was headed by a Mr Hamilton and offered trips on the Fal, the Percuil River and in Falmouth Bay. The local manager was Bart Moore of Mylor, once a neighbour of the Newmans. There were three Green Boats, the launches *Temptress*, *Tamar*, and *Gondolier* (ex-Victory Pleasures Ltd). They were joined in 1962 by the ex-Newman *Skylark II*.

During the early 1950s, George Pill built his own passenger boat, the *White Lady*. His brothers, Gerald and Kenneth, also owned passenger launches. Vessels associated with the Pill family have included the *Water Spry* (ex-Victory Pleasures Ltd), the *Tamar Belle*—a Turnchapel-built, ex-steam boat of 1905 which once operated on the River Yealm as the *Kitley Belle*—and the launch *Rebecca*.

During the 1950s and 1960s the launch *Marina* specialised in offering trips to the Helford. Later a 48ft ex-Poole launch, the *Marina II*, plied to Frenchman's Creek and offered Saturday morning trips viewing Falmouth's waterfront. A guide produced in conjunction with Falmouth Civic Society was designed with this cruise in mind. During the late 1970s, the *Marina II* and the *Rebecca* (ex-Pill, ex-Colin Warren) were owned briefly by P.A. Lochrie. The *Marina II* is now at Torquay.

A.S. Cook bought the little twin screw private yacht *Evelina* from Stanley Kearie, a Falmouth butcher, in 1950. The motor vessel measured just 10t.g., 34 x 9·5 x 5·2ft and maintained Stan Cook's 'Roseland Cruise' until she was sold to a Newton Ferrers fisherman in 1965. Her replacement was a larger 100 seater motor vessel named *Evelina II*. During the 1970s Stephen Jones bought the *Evelina II* and in 1975 exchanged her for the ex-Harry John launch *Kingsley*, which was in the Isles of Scilly. Thus the *Evelina II* survives in the Isles of Scilly as the *Kingsley II*.

Joseph Timmins of Ponsharden, a Trinity House pilot, was running the launch *Scotia* in the 1950s. He later added the *Queen of Helford*, a sister to both the *Skylark II* and the *Temptress*. In 1962 Joseph and Sidney Timmins took delivery of their new Blackmore built motor vessel, the *Queen of Helford*. Until she was sold to George Riddals of Dartmouth in 1976, the *Queen of Helford* specialised in offering trips to the river after which she had been named.

Harry Johns, meanwhile, continued to consolidate the Truro trade and in 1962 had built by Blackmores of Bideford a new 60ft motor vessel, the *Enterprise III*. In the following year the North Devon boatbuilders completed a third vessel for Harry Johns. The new boat inherited the name *Enterprise* from Johns' earlier passenger launch. The MV *Queen of the Fal* was sold in the same year to R.D. & J.H. Paynter of St Ives, from which port she still plies, renamed the *Cornish Belle*. She was succeeded on the Fal by another, smaller, launch, which also bore the name *Queen of the Fal*. In 1964 H.S.A. Johns and his son Alisdair incorporated the company Fal Pleasure Cruises Ltd. Included amongst the shareholders was Francis Berryman and later Frank Anthony, both pleasure boat skippers. Harry Johns died in 1971, but Alisdair Johns and Fal Pleasure Cruises Ltd. continues to operate the immaculately-maintained fleet of 'Enterprise' boats. A timetabled service is provided during the summer months between Falmouth and Worth's Quay. At low tide the river journey terminates at Malpas, where a pontoon landing is now available, and the trip to Truro is completed aboard a minibus, which meets each 'Enterprise' boat—not so very different from a century before, when under similar circumstances a wagonette met the steamers of Benney & Co.

The Green Boat fleet of the River Fal & Western Cruises Co Ltd. was sold off in the 1970s. George Pill bought the *Gondolier*. The sister launches *Skylark II* and the *Temptress* were taken over by Bob Rogers who worked them in competition with the Pill family. George Pill later took over the two launches and sold the *Temptress* to Kenneth Pill who operated angling trips with her until she was sold to Millbrook owners in 1985. She has since changed ownership within the port of Plymouth and been renamed the *Condor*. The Aberystwyth built, ex-Fleetwood motor vessel, *May Queen*, was purchased by the Pill family in 1968 to work a St Mawes ferry service following the demise of the St Mawes Steam Tug & Passenger Co.Ltd. In 1974 William George Pill, William Jenking and George Henry Pill, incorporated the Cornish Ferry (Red Funnel) Co.Ltd. The first action of the new Company was to purchase the *St Gerrans* from her London owners. Considerable local interest was aroused when she returned to the Fal. Although in an appalling condition, the old St Mawes ferry boat was overhauled and repainted during the 1974/5 winter and returned to service for the following season—revisiting her old haunts on the Helford River. Other boats associated with members of the Pill family at this time were: the *Devon Belle* of 1922 (ex-Millbrook Steamboat & Trading Co.Ltd) and an ex-Southampton motor launch, renamed the *Tamar Belle*. In addition to those boats directly connected with the Cornish Ferry (Red Funnel) Co Ltd., Kenneth Pill was independently running the launches *Queen of Falmouth* and the *Champion*. In 1978 he joined the three directors of the Cornish Ferry (Red Funnel) Co.Ltd to form a new company, the Falmouth Passenger Boat Co.Ltd. Subsequent vessels associated with the joint companies have included: the motor launch *Skylark II* (ex-Newman, ex-Green Boats, sold 1984 to R. Elworthy of Millbrook); the 21t.g. *Westminster Belle* (ex-Thames, sold 1985 to Looe Cruises & Ferry, sold again 1987 to Millbrook owners); the 91t.g. saloon vessel *Tudor Prince* (ex-Torbay Prince, built by Blackmores in 1947, came to Falmouth in 1981); and the *Princessa* of 1921 (ex-Portsmouth Harbour ferry, ex-Blue Funnel Cruises of Southampton.). In common with the character of

the Pill family themselves, their fleet livery might best be described as colourful. While the family has endured its share of differences with local authorities and fellow operators, their passengers have continued to enjoy trips to the Helford aboard the veteran *St Gerrans*, which, until 1988, has been the only passenger vessel still to run to the river. Excursions on the Fal itself are conducted by the *Tudor Prince* and/or the *Princessa*. The start of the 1988 season has unfortunately seen the Pill family in dispute with Carrick District Council and their boats officially banned from the Prince of Wales Pier. At time of writing the long-serving *St Gerrans* has reportedly been sold to a buyer in the north.

Due to the need for rationalisation in this review of post war motor vessels, it is acknowledged. that some of the smaller owner-skippered craft remain unrecorded. It would be unfair however, having listed all other current passenger vessels, to ignore the two remaining independent operators. E.R. Penrose's 42ft motor launch, *Look Ahead*, offers excursions from St Mawes Quay. In addition, various smaller boats, each with a licence for twelve passengers, continue a long tradition of watermen's trips from St Mawes. Kenneth Pill, jnr runs the *Temptress II* (ex-*Kentish Lady*) on harbour trips from the Prince of Wales Pier—viewing Falmouth Docks, St Anthony Head, the Percuil River and Flushing.

The history of the Fal's passenger 'steamers' cannot yet be concluded, their story is set to run for as long as holidaymakers continue to visit Cornwall. The story of the River Fal's passenger boat trade predates Cornwall's railways and the later invasion of motor road transport. Whilst the massive civil engineering works associated with the rail and road systems have transformed areas of the County beyond recognition, a waterborne traveller from a century ago would experience little difficulty in recognising any one reach of the Fal's waterways today. The steam passenger tugs have long since disappeared from the waters of the Falmouth district, but the distinctive and varied coastline around the beautiful Fal estuary looks very much the same when viewed from the decks of their present day counterparts.

The *St Gerrans* in the Carrick Roads in 1963.
Photo: Ivor Ireland

The *New Roseland, en route* to Falmouth in 1963.

Photo: Ivor Ireland

The *St Mawes Castle* and the *New Roseland* at the Prince of Wales Pier, c1950. Astern of the *New Roseland*, beside the pier is the Fairmile 'B' launch, the *Pendennis*, which was on charter to the Falmouth Boat Building Company. The other launch is H Johns' original *Enterprise*.

Keith Handcock collection

King Harry Reach, c1950. The *St Mawes Castle* heads downstream while the chain ferry approaches the Feock side. Having been introduced in 1913, this floating bridge was virtually worn out when this photograph was taken. Ferry No 3, an ex-Saltash chain bridge, should have replaced No 2 in 1933 but was found unsuitable. Relief eventually came in 1951 in the shape of Ferry No 4, an ex-landing craft converted by Holman's of Penzance. This bridge was almost wrecked on the Lizard Peninsula during her delivery trip, sustaining damage which cost £12,000 to repair. No 4 was replaced by another ex-Saltash ferry during the 1960s, which in turn was succeeded by the present chain bridge in 1974. No 6 was built by Dredge Marine Ltd of Ponshaden.

Photo: Roy Stribley collection

The *New Princess Maud* in 1963.
Photo: Ivor Ireland

Rodney Newman's launch, the
Freelance, pictured alongside a ship laid up
on the Fal. The *Freelance* is remembered as
a very fast boat.
Photo: courtesy Peter Newman

The Newman's *Skylark II* at Worth's Quay. An ex-Admiralty launch with a very strong diagonally built, double hull, the *Skylark II* still offers river trips at Plymouth.

Photo: courtesy Peter Newman

The Tresillian River at Malpas during the 1950s. Moored offshore is the *Skylark II* (nearest the river bank) and Harryenry John's MV *Queen of the Fal*, the largest boat in the group.

Roy Stribley collection

Peter Newman has a series of photographs depicting the conversion of the *Skylark of Tolverne*, by his brother George, from a virtual hulk to a certificated passenger vessel, during the 1950s. That the Newmans' pride in the result was justified, is evidenced in this lovely photograph of the boat, taken at Falmouth. George Newman is at the helm.

Photo: courtesy Peter Newman

A selection of the boats operating at Falmouth in 1954.
left to right: The *Skylark of Tolverne* during her first season; the *Skylark*; *Temptress*—offering a trip to Coverack at 2.30PM; the *Marina II* for the Helford River, Frenchman's Creek and Port Navas to land; and on the end of the row, either the *Sea Horse* or the *Merry Widow.*
back row, left to right: first boat, unidentified; the second vessel is the Timmins' *Scotia*; Stan Cook's *Evelina*—for 'the Roseland Cruise'; the *Marina* (I); and finally the *Y Not*, operated by Messrs Cox and Barnes.

A K collection

H Johns' first motor launch to carry the name *Queen of the Fal*.
Photo: courtesy Peter Newman

April 22nd 1969. Robin Knox-Johnson sails his ketch *Suhali* into Falmouth as the first person to circumnavigate the world non-stop and single handed. Numbered among the welcoming flotilla is the *Enterprise II*.
Osborne's of Falmouth

The *New Princess Maud* in 1986, passing the oil platform *Ocean Kokuei*, which was laid up in the Carrick Roads during 1985/86.

Photo: A K

Ticket kiosk on St Mawes Quay.

The *Nankersey* in 1987 with Greenbank Quay in the background.

Photo: A K

The *Princess Maria* in 1987, departing from Prince of Wales Pier. The new quayside development in the background, romantically titled the 'Packet Quays', is built upon the foreshore once known as Admiral's Quay, which included the boatyard of Burt & Son amongst its many commercial premises. The properties on the right are built upon quays which were constructed during the 18th century.

Photo: A K

The Flushing Ferry in 1987. The new ferry boat *Miranda* approaches the Prince of Wales Pier with Flushing in the background.

Photo: A K

Following a quiet cream tea at Tolverne Cottage, Peter Newman returns his trippers aboard the *Heather* along the less quiet waters of the Fal, to Town Quay, Falmouth in 1987.

Photo: A K

Kenneth Pill (jnr.) at the helm of his motor vessel, the *Temptress II*, in 1987.

Photo: A K

The *Devon Belle* was built as the *Marie* in Berlin in 1922. Between 1927–1979 she was owned by the Millbrook Steamboat & Trading Co Ltd on the River Tamar. The steel motor vessel was acquired by the Cornish Ferry (Red Funnel) Co Ltd to operate excursions on the Fal. The *Devon Belle* was sold to Southsea owners in 1987.

Photo: A K

The *May Queen* maintains a seasonal ferry
service between St Mawes and Town Quay
in Falmouth. She is pictured here crossing
the Carrick Roads during 1984.

Photo: A K

The *Tamar Belle* usually works from Town
Quay, providing short trips to Tolverne.
Photo: A K

The *Princessa* arrived at Falmouth in 1987 to
maintain River Fal trips. She was originally a
steam powered Portsmouth Harbour ferry
boat, built in 1921. The long serving
St Gerrans, seen here approaching, is only
six years her junior. Both boats wear the
livery of the Pill family's Cornish Ferry (Red
Funnel) Ltd.

Photo: A K

The *Enterprise* in Falmouth Harbour, 1987.
Photo: A K

The *Enterprise II* approaching Worth's Quay in 1984. The warehouses of Phoenix (or Trafalgar) Wharf in the background have enjoyed something of a revival in recent years. Amongst others, the wharf is home to Radio Cornwall and Blewetts Bakery.
Photo: A K

The spotless *Enterprise III* in the Carrick
Roads in 1987. She is following the channel
across from St Just Pool to the opposite
shore near Restronguet Point.

Photo: A K

APPENDIX ONE

STEAMERS OF THE ST MAWES STEAM TUG & PASSENGER CO LTD & OTHER ST MAWES FERRY OPERATORS

ST MAWES STEAM TUG AND PASSENGER CO LTD

Name	Type	Year	Tonnage	Dimensions	Builder	Engine
WOTTON	IRON S.S.	1866 1869 1896	28·46	64·0 12·25 6·05	H H PRICE Neath Abbey, Swansea	Compound diagonal (1882)
JANE	WOOD S.S.	1872 1876 1888	16·38	46·8 12·7 5·3	JOSEPH OSBORNE Newquay	WILLIAMS' PERRAN FOUNDRY (HILL FOUNDRY, Gerrans, 1882)
ROSELAND	STEEL S.S.	1886 1886 1946	41	72·9 13·5 6·7	COX & Co Falmouth	Triple expansion COX & CO, Falmouth
PRINCESS MAY	STEEL S.S.	1894 1894 1902	66	76·9 16·6 6·9	COX & Co Falmouth	Triple expansion COX & CO, Falmouth
ALEXANDRA	STEEL S.S.	1902 1902 1916	73	84·6 16·9 7·7	COX & Co Falmouth	Triple expansion COX & CO, Falmouth
ST MAWES	STEEL S.S.	1917 1917 1942	80	75·6 18·0 7·6	COX & Co Falmouth	Triple expansion COX & CO, Falmouth
ST GERRANS	STEEL M.V.	1927 1927 1968	73	69·25 17·35 5·5	COX & Co Falmouth	Semi-diesel Gardiner
BERRY CASTLE	WOOD M.V.	c1930	–	–		–
NEW ROSELAND	STEEL M.V.	1935 1938 1968	59	69·6 17·1 5·4·	COOK, WELTON & GEMMELL Beverley, Hull	4 stroke int. combustion BERGUIS CO, Glasgow
ST MAWES CASTLE	STEEL M.V.	1948 1948 1968	75	70·0 18·2 6·0	PHILIP & SON Dartmouth	BLACKSTONE & CO, London
NEW PRINCESS MAUD	WOOD M.V.	1950 1950 1970	9	52·0	London	–

ST MAWES FERRY CO LTD *and SUCCESIVE OPERATORS*

Name	Type	Year	Tonnage	Dimensions	Builder	Engine
NEW PRINCESS MAUD	WOOD M.V.	1950 1970 ext	–	–	as above	–
PRINCESS MARINA	WOOD M.V.	c1970	–	52·0	–	–
PRINCESS MARIA	WOOD M.V.	c1970 ext	–	48·0	–	–
NANKERSEY	WOOD M.V.	1951 1976 ext	23	45·0 13·8 5·7	FALMOUTH BOAT CONSTRUCTION	Diesel BERGUIS CO, Glasgow

ROSELAND & FALMOUTH STEAM PACKET CO LTD

Name	Type	Year	Tonnage	Dimensions	Builder	Engine
ST MAWES CASTLE	WOOD M.V.	1887 1887 1891	48 53 (1888)	75·0 15·1 6·3	HARVEY & Co Hayle	Compound inverted HARVEY FOUNDRY
FALMOUTH CASTLE	IRON S.S.	1889 1889 1891	24	55·8 13·2 5·8	Wm HENRY LEAN Falmouth	Compound inverted LEAN (1883)

STEAMERS OF THE RIVER FAL STEAMSHIP CO LTD & ASSOCIATED OPERATORS

NAME	TYPE	BUILT AQU'D DISP'D	TONS GROSS	LENGTH WIDTH DEPTH	BUILDER	ENGINES & BUILDER
PHILIP THOMAS						
RAPID	WOOD S.S.	1872 1872 1879	60	67·0 16·7 8·8	JOHN STEPHENS Charlestown	–
ALBERT	IRON S.S.	1876 1876 1878	65	77·1 16·7 9·3	COX, FARLEY & Co Falmouth	Compound inverted WILLIAMS' PERRAN FOUNDRY
ALBERT	IRON S.S.	1877 1878 1879	79	82·3 17·6 9·7	COX, FARLEY & Co Falmouth	Compound inverted WILLIAMS' PERRAN FOUNDRY
ALBERT	WOOD S.S.	1879 1879 1881	40	71·5 14·7 7·4	JOHN STEPHENS Feock	Inverted WILLIAMS' PERRAN FOUNDRY
EMPEROR	IRON S.S.	1882 1882 1883	–	85·8	–	–
EMPEROR	IRON S.S.	1883 1883 1903	114·26	90·0	HARVEY & Co Hayle	HAYLE FOUNDRY
WILLIAM J THOMAS & FAMILY						
VICTOR	STEEL S.S.	1898 1898 1934	153	106·0 20·0 11·3	POOL, SKINNER & WILLIAMS Falmouth	Triple expansion COX & CO, Falmouth
W J THOMAS & A W CHARD (THE RIVER FAL STEAMSHIP COMPANY, from 1901)						
VICTORIA	STEEL T.S.S.	1900 1900 1900	67·74	82·0 17·4 6·7	COX & Co Falmouth	2 x Compound inverted COX & CO, Falmouth
VICTORIA	STEEL T.S.S.	1901 1901 1905	67·82	85·0 18·1 6·4	COX & Co Falmouth	2 x Compound inverted COX & CO, Falmouth
BENNEY & COMPANY						
RESOLUTE	WOOD S.S.	1877 1877 1902	32	63·6 14·25 6·31	SCOBLE & DAVIES Malpas	Compound inverted COX & CO, Falmouth
NEW RESOLUTE	WOOD S.S.	1882 1882 1906	39·77	71·25 15·1 6·7	SCOBLE & DAVIES Malpas	Inverted COX & CO, Falmouth
QUEEN OF THE FAL	STEEL S.S.	1893 1893 1906	62·06	81·6 16·7 7·2	COX & Co Falmouth	Compound inverted COX & CO, Falmouth
RIVER FAL STEAMSHIP CO LTD (1906)						
NEW RESOLUTE	WOOD S.S.	1882 1906 1927	–	–	as above	–
QUEEN OF THE FAL	STEEL S.S.	1893 1906 1911	–	–	as above	–
PRINCESS VICTORIA	STEEL T.S.S.	1907 1907 1942	67·48	81·5 18·8 6·5	COX & Co Falmouth	2 x Compound inverted COX & CO, Falmouth
QUEEN OF THE FAL	STEEL S.S.	1912 1912 1942	71	81·0 18·5 7·0	COX & Co Falmouth	Compound inverted COX & CO, Falmouth

APPENDIX TWO

—Waterline profile drawings of Cox & Co/Silley Cox built passenger steamers of the River Fal Steamship Co Ltd and the St Mawes Steam Tug & Passenger Co Ltd.

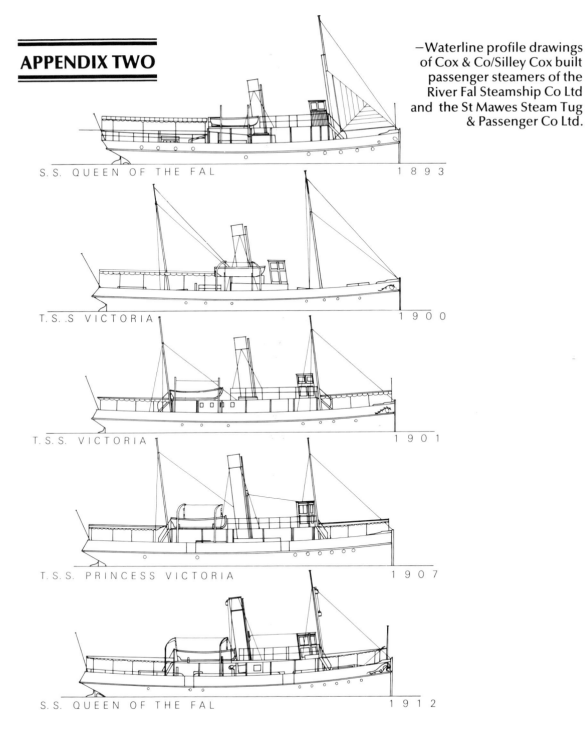

S.S. QUEEN OF THE FAL   1893

T.S..S VICTORIA   1900

T.S.S. VICTORIA   1901

T.S.S. PRINCESS VICTORIA   1907

S.S. QUEEN OF THE FAL   1912

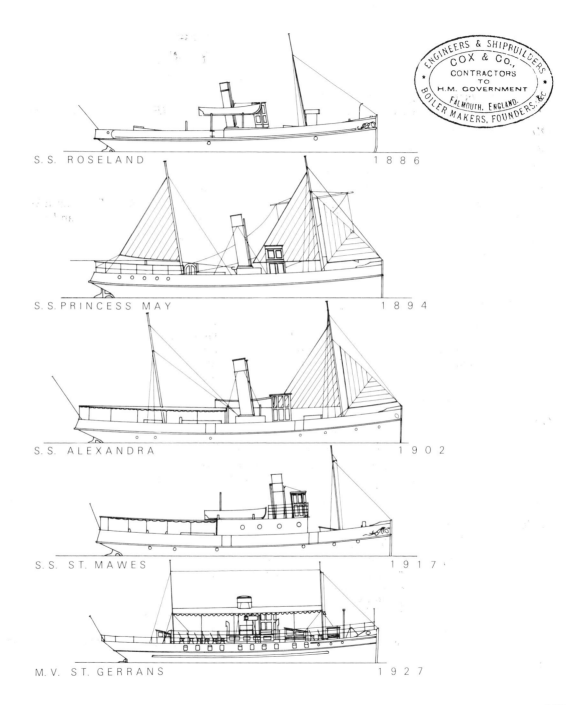

ENGINEERS & SHIPBUILDERS
COX & Co.,
CONTRACTORS
TO
H.M. GOVERNMENT
FALMOUTH, ENGLAND.
BOILER MAKERS, FOUNDERS, &c.

S.S. ROSELAND   1 8 8 6

S.S. PRINCESS MAY   1 8 9 4

S.S. ALEXANDRA   1 9 0 2

S.S. ST. MAWES   1 9 1 7

M.V. ST. GERRANS   1 9 2 7

APPENDIX THREE

GENERAL REGISTER & RECORD OFFICE OF SHIPPING & SEAMEN
OFFICAL LOG BOOK & ACCOUNT OF VOYAGES & CREW OF A VESSEL LESS THAN 80 TONS REGISTER

QUEEN OF THE FAL

Offical No: 114925   Port of Registry: Truro.   71·30 tons gross

Half year: January 1st 1913 — June 30th 1913.

Managing Owner: A E Benney and W J Thomas, Market Street, Falmouth.
Draught of water in salt water at time of proceeding to sea: Forward 3·6ft. Aft 6·0ft. Freeboard: 3ft.
Trade: Towing and carrying passengers from Falmouth to ports within the limits of Looe and Penzance.

Crew:	George Stoddern	Portscatho	Master
	James Cornelius Benney	Falmouth	Engineer
	Charles Riddle	Falmouth	Engineer
	Richard Benney	Truro	A.B.

Crew discharged on 13th April 1913

	Albert Edward Benney	Truro	Master
	Frederick Thomas	Perranwell	Engineer
	Joseph Vincent	St Mawes	Mate
	John Henry Drew	Falmouth	Stoker
	Frederick Detain	France	Seaman

All joined the ship on 14th April 1913.

On the dates: April 14,15,17,22.
May 7,12,13,17,26,27,29.
June 2,5,9,12,13,14,17,18,19,20,23,24,26,28,30.

William Richards, Penryn was Master Cert. No 039430
Richard Veall, Camborne was Engineer Cert. No 037905 1st Class

Half year: July 1st 1913 — December 31st 1913.

Trade: as above plus extended No 3 limits between Plymouth and Penzance.
Nov 1st 1913 — Dec 31st 1913 laid up at Falmouth.

On the dates: July 3,5,7,8,9,11,14,17,18,19,21,22,28,29,31.
August 2,5,6,8,9,11,14,15,19,21,22,23,25,27,28.
September 2,5,6,8,10,11,18,19,22,25,26.
October 3,8,9
William Richards was Master and Richard Veall was Engineer.
William Richards discharged August 30th 1913.
James Shaw, Falmouth signed on as Master Cert No 6940, on 2nd September 1913.

Crew discharged October 31st 1913.

GENERAL REGISTER & RECORD OFFICE OF SHIPPING & SEAMEN
OFFICAL LOG BOOK & ACCOUNT OF VOYAGES & CREW OF A VESSEL LESS THAN 80 TONS REGISTER
ALEXANDRA:

Official No: 117981   Port of Registry: Falmouth   72·69 tons gross. 23·51 tons net.   49·7 H P

Half year: January 1st—June 30th 1913.
Managing Owner: W P Hugo Rowe, 6 Market Street, Falmouth.
Master: Charles Nicholls, Portscatho, Certificate No 03148.
Draught of water in salt water at time of proceeding to sea: Forward 4·6ft. Aft 6·3ft.
Trade: laid up from January 1st to May 11th 1913 at Falmouth.
        From May 12th to June 30th 1913 employed on passenger excursions on route:
        Falmouth Harbour between limits of Lizard Point and Fowey.
Signed: Edward Jenking—(as Master and owner).

Crew:	Charles Nichols	Portscatho	12.5.13	Master (certificated)
	Edward Jenking	St Mawes	1.1.13	Master and Mate
	Albert Hitchens	St Mawes	1.1.13	Engineer
	Arthur Lower	Weston-super- Mare	1.1.13	A.B.
	James Bellman	St Mawes	1.1.13	Fireman
	Wilfred Richards	Falmouth	12.5.13	Engineer Cert No 45392 2nd Class.

On the dates   May 12,14,16,27,28.
                 June 3,7,11,12,13,16,17,19,23,24,26.
                 Charles Nichols was Master and W Richards was Engineer.
                 All other dates from 12th May 1913 to 30th June 1913 E Jenking was Master.

Half year: July 1st 1913—December 31st 1913.

Managing Owner: St Mawes Tug & Passenger Co Ltd, Falmouth.
Trade: From July to October making passenger excursions on route:
        Falmouth Harbour between limits of Penzance and Fowey.
        At other dates Passenger service between Falmouth and St Mawes.
        December 2nd 1913—December 31st 1913 laid up at Falmouth.

Crew discharged:
        2.10.13   Charles Nichols
        2.10.13   Edward Jenking signed off as Mate
        continues Albert Hitchens
        2.12.13   Arthur Lower
        2.12.13   James Bellman
        2.12.13   Wilfred Richards
        continues   Edward Jenking re-signed on as Master

From July 10th 1913 this vessel makes excursions from Falmouth to the limits Penzance and Fowey and on these occasions a Certificated Master and Engineer are carried. At other times the vessel is engaged within the limits of the Harbour, when Jenking and Hitchens only are employed.

APPENDIX FOUR

EXCURSION PROGRAMME, WEEK ENDING AUGUST 23rd 1913

	VICTOR	ALEXANDRA	NEW RESOLUTE	QUEEN OF THE FAL	PRINCESS VICTORIA	ROSELAND
Monday 18th	LIZARD	St JUST (morn.) TRESILLIAN RIVER & GATLEY'S QUAY (aft.)	St JUST (morn.) St JUST (aft.)	HELFORD (morn.) GWEEK QUAY (aft.)	MALPAS & TRURO	St MAWES, St ANTHONY & PERCUIL
Tuesday 19th	COVERACK REGATTA	HELFORD RIVER (morn.) HELFORD RIVER & PORT NAVAS QUAY (aft.)	St ANTHONY LIGHTHOUSE & MYLOR	LIZARD & COVERACK	MALPAS & TRURO	St MAWES, St ANTHONY & PERCUIL
Wednesday 20th	–	LIZARD & PENZANCE	St JUST (morn.) ROUNDWOOD QUAY (aft.)	HELFORD (morn.) PORT NAVAS & GWEEK (aft)	MALPAS & TRURO	St MAWES, St ANTHONY & PERCUIL
Thursday 21st	LIZARD	MEVAGISSEY & FOWEY	LOE BEACH	MEVAGISSEY & FOWEY	MALPAS & TRURO	St MAWES, St ANTHONY & PERCUIL
Friday 22nd	FOWEY	HELFORD RIVER (morn.) HELFORD RIVER (aft.)	HARBOUR & MYLOR	COVERACK (morn.) COVERACK & PORTHOUSTOCK (aft.)	MALPAS & TRURO	St MAWES, St ANTHONY & PERCUIL
Saturday 23rd	MANACLES	HELFORD RIVER (morn.) HELFORD RIVER (aft.)	HARBOUR & St JUST	COVERACK, LIZARD & PENZANCE	MALPAS & TRURO	St MAWES, St ANTHONY & PERCUIL

Princess Victoria
at the Prince of Wales Pier.

A K collection

BIBLIOGRAPHY, SOURCES & ACKNOWLEDGEMENTS

I must first acknowledge the information contained within the late Graham Farr's book *West Country Passenger Steamers* (Stephenson, 1970). Whilst many of Mr Farr's sources have been re-examined and expanded upon, his chapter on the Fal's steamers provided valuable assistance for this history.

Official documents consulted included the Custom House Shipping Registers of Falmouth and Truro. Seven of the Registers: Falmouth 1843-56, 1856-66, 1866-84; Truro 1824-48, 1848-55, 1855-1909, and Falmouth Shipping Transactions 1849-97, are held in the County Records Office, Truro. The balance of Shipping and Transaction Registers, covering the two ports up to date, are kept at the Custon House, Falmouth and I thank the Librarian and Archivist, HM Customs & Excise, London, and Mr John Bennet, the Registrar of Shipping at Customs House, Falmouth, for permission to view these Registers. Log sheets of the General Register of Shipping and Seamen are also held in the County Record Office. Although only a small sample is available, in some instances just one annual return, the selection is comprehensive and includes most of the passenger steamers mentioned in this book. Records of the relevant incorporated passenger boat companies which are still held at the Company Records Office, Cardiff, were also consulted.

In addition to Graham Farr's book, other publications which impart information concerning the Fal's steamers and other associated Westcountry passenger vessels are: *British Steam Tugs* by P N Thomas (Waine Research Publications, 1983); *Trip Out*, passenger boat guides, 1977 to date, compiled and published by Geoffrey Hamer; *Passenger Steamers of the River Tamar* by Alan Kittridge (Twelveheads Press, 1984); *Passenger Steamers of the River Dart* by Richard Clammer and Alan Kittridge (Twelveheads Press, 1987); *King Harry Steam Ferry Co Ltd, 1888–1988* by L D Champion and V H Simmons-Hodge (K H S F Co Ltd, 1988). Information about the two ex-Oreston & Turnchapel Steamboat Co Ltd Flushing ferry boats, was obtained from the minute books of that company, courtesy of Mary Anthony and David Elford. Cornwall Records Office File No AD 140 holds papers relating to the Flushing ferry back to 1660. Details of the steamers' excursion programmes, throughout the years, were gained from the pages of Lake's *Falmouth Packet & Cornwall Advertiser* which is kept on microfilm in the Cornwall Local Studies Library, Redruth and as hard copies in Falmouth Library.

Peter Newman of Tolverne Cottage has guided me through the complicated history of the post war period, provided details of his own family's vessels and lent photographs of boats that were operating during the 1950s and 60s. Both Peter Newman and George Pill read the manuscript of Chapter 5, but any errors remain my own.

Amongst the books which record the maritime history of the River Fal during the 19th and 20th centuries, Basil Greenhill's classic book *The Merchant Schooners* (2 volumes: David & Charles, reprinted 1978 by National Maritime Museum), appears alone in providing a valuable account of the Estuary's shipbuilders and trading vessels. Other maritime books consulted include: *Westcountry Coasting Ketches* by W J Slade and Basil Greenhill (Conway Maritime Press, 1974); *The Packet Captains of Flushing* by M E Philbrick; *The Lizard & Cadgwith Lifeboat* (R N L I) and *The Story of Cornwall's Ports and Harbours* (Tor Mark Press, 1970).

The Redruth & Chasewater Railway by D B Barton (Bradford Barton, 2nd edition, 1978), was the source of much information concerning the paddle tugs of that company and the industrial history of Restronguet Creek, Devoran and other mineral quays. Similarly helpful were: *A History of Copper Mining in Cornwall and Devon* by D B Barton (Bradford Barton, 3rd edition, 1978) and *The Harvey's of Hayle* by Edmund Vale (Bradford Barton, 1966). An article entitled 'The Falmouth Branch', by Alan Bennet, made a useful and timely appearance in *Railway World* magazine, June 1987.

My knowledge of the district's topography and history has been improved by reading: *Old Cornish Bridges and Streams* by Charles Henderson and Henry Coates (Bradford Barton, reprint 1972); Pictorial Booklet for the Tercentenary of Falmouth by Rosalind Beckett (Falmouth Borough Council, 1962); *Falmouth's Famous Past* by Bob Dunstan (1968); *Bygone Truro* by Shelia Bird (Phillmore,

1986); Murray's *Guide to Devon & Cornwall (David & Charles reprint, 1971); The Official Falmouth Guide, 1910/ 1920/1930/1947; Falmouth Guide by Edwin T Olver, 1905/ 1912/1914; The Falmouth Packet Guide*, published by Lean's Falmouth Packet, 1950; Burrows Pocket Guide 1910/1920; Ward Lock Falmouth Guide 1920/1930; and the St Mawes Steam Tug & Passenger Co's Handbook for 1930. For the loan of a majority of the guide books listed above I thank John Stengelhofen.

The photographers where known and/or the copyright holders of each print used, are credited throughout the book. These pictures constitute an invaluable part of this history and I thank the Royal Institution of Cornwall and its Curator, Roger Penhallurick, for permission to search their extensive photographic collection. I am particularly indebted to Roy Stribley of Truro for putting his photographic collection at my disposal and for affording me the benefit of his local knowledge of both the river and its passenger craft. Many of the photographs which are reproduced were originally taken by E A Bragg of Falmouth. His postcards were sold aboard the steamers and it is particularly fortunate that his 'Peeps on the Fal' series and other river and coastal views usually included as a theme, one of the Fal's passenger vessels.

Additional photographs were lent by P N Thomas, Mr H L- Martin, John Clarkson, Ivor Ireland, Keith Handcock, Falmouth Library—courtesy of Mrs Pauline Staite—and Stephen Rowson.

Finally I thank Ted and Betty Messenger at Chy Mengleth for their invaluable work behind the scenes and Lindy Stengelhofen for transcribing the manuscript onto computer disc.

Pictured aboard the *Roseland* during the early 1920s. If the postcard caption, 'A regular passenger at 96' is true, then this gentleman was about five years old when the coastal paddler, *Sir Francis Drake*, brought news of the Reform Bill to Falmouth in 1832.
A K collection

INDEX OF PASSENGER VESSELS

Queen of Helford MV (1962) **75 92**
Queen of the Fal SS (1893) **46 53 57 58 59 65 66 67 68 75
79 83 84 111 112**
Queen of the Fal SS (1911) **1 36 47 59 60 71 73 75 76 77
78 79 81 83 87 89 111 112 114 116**
Queen of the Fal MV **91 92 98 101**
Queen of the Fal (2) MV **92**
Rapid SS **9 15 111**
Rebecca MV **92**
Resolute SS **6 7 12 16 23 31 37 57 58**
Robina TSS **77**
Roseland SS **1 4 34 35 37 39 40 41 43 44 47 51 53 59
60 66 76 89 110 113 116**
Rosetta SS **17**
Royal Cambria PS **13**
St David PS **13**
St Gerrans MV **36 37 49 75 76 89 93 94 107 110 113**
St Keverne SS **15 16 33**
St Mawes SS **36 37 48 49 59 60 85 89 110 113**
St Mawes Castle SS **34 35 41 110**
St Mawes Castle MV **89 95 96 110**
Sea Horse MV **100**
Scotia MV **92 100**
Shannon PS **12 14 28**
Sheppy Queen MV **91**
Sir Francis Drake PS **9 13 14 15**

Sir Richard Grenville TSS **76 86**
Skylark MV **91 100**
Skylark II MV **91 92 93**
Skylark of Tolverne MV **8 91 99 100**
Sydney PS **10 11 28**
Tamar MV **92**
Tamar Belle MV (1905) **92 107**
Tamar Belle MV **93**
Temptress MV **92 93 100**
Temptress II MV **93 105**
Thames PS **13**
Truro Belle SS **17 38 52**
Tudor Prince MV **88 93**
Victor SS (1875) **15 16 55**
Victor SS (1898) **1 17 30 55 56 57 58 60 61 62 73 75 76 77
78 82 84 111 116**
Victoria TSS (L&SWRly) **76**
Victoria TSS (1900) **36 56 57 63 111 112**
Victoria TSS (1901) **53 56 57 58 64 66 111 112**
Viking MV **31**
Water Spry MV **91 92**
Waverley PS **77**
Westminster Belle MV **93**
White Lady MV **92**
William Fawcett PS **13**
Wotton SS **9 15 16 29 33 34 35 36 110**
Y Not MV **100**

The vessels of the St Mawes Steam Tug & Passenger Co Ltd, beautifully reproduced as waterline models by Roy Stribley of Truro. From right to left: the *Roseland, Princess May, Alexandra, St Mawes, St Gerrans, New Roseland* and the *St Mawes Castle*.